IT'S JUST A
PHASE
SO DON'T MISS IT

WHY EVERY LIFE STAGE OF A KID MATTERS

**AND AT LEAST 13 THINGS YOUR CHURCH
SHOULD DO ABOUT IT**

REGGIE JOINER & KRISTEN IVY

orange

ORANGE BOOKS

IT'S JUST A PHASE, SO DON'T MISS IT:
WHY EVERY LIFE STAGE OF A KID MATTERS,
AND AT LEAST 13 THINGS YOUR CHURCH SHOULD DO ABOUT IT

www.justaphase.com
Published by Orange, a division of The reThink Group, Inc.,
5870 Charlotte Lane, Suite 300, Cumming, GA 30040 U.S.A.

Scripture quotations marked NLT are taken from the Holy Bible, New
Living Translation, Copyright 1996. Used by permission of Tyndale House
Publishers, Inc., Wheaton, Illinois 60189.

All other Scripture quotations, unless otherwise noted, are taken from the
Holy Bible, New International Version®. NIV®. Copyright © 1973, 1978,
1984 by International Bible Society. Used by permission of Zondervan.

Other Orange products are available online and direct from the publisher.
Visit our website at www.ThinkOrange.com for more resources like these.
ISBN: 978-1-941259-43-6

©2015 Reggie Joiner and Kristen Ivy
Authors: Reggie Joiner and Kristen Ivy
Lead Editor: Mike Jeffries

Art Direction: Ryan Boon
Project Manager: Nate Brandt
Series Editor: Karen Wilson
Book Design: FiveStone

Printed in the United States of America
First Edition 2015
7 8 9 10 11 12 13 14 15 16

10/26/20

FROM REGGIE JOINER:

To my mother, Dee.

For believing in me at every phase and seeing in me what no one else sees.

To my Aunt Geneva (Nennie) Bray.

For raising my mom and proving to me that God is real.
Your lifetime of prayers impacted me in more ways than I will ever know,
and the food around here hasn't tasted nearly as good since you left.

FROM KRISTEN IVY

To my mother, Cindy.

For raising me through every phase—some of which tested both of us—and
for sharing with me both your faith in God and your love of children.

To my Grandma Street.

For leaving a legacy of learning and love in each of your four
children, seven grandchildren and 13+ great-grandchildren.
We all look forward to the day we will see you again.

ENDORSEMENTS

One thing that robs kids of their childhood is the phrase, "I can't wait until . . ." In a culture where everybody wants to hurry through to what is next, *It's Just a Phase* presses pause and reminds leaders to pay attention to what's critical in every stage so kids will know they matter.

CAZ MCCASLIN
PRESIDENT & FOUNDER, UPWARD SPORTS

This is a crash course in child development that could radically change the way the church relates to kids and teenagers. Kristen Ivy, Reggie Joiner, and the Orange team have once again done the hard research and work to make it easier for the rest of us.

SHERRY SURRATT
CEO, MOPS INTERNATIONAL

If you are a youth leader, you need to study both Scripture and your students. Ivy and Joiner have given us an amazing tool to transfer sound theology to the hearts of the next generation, one phase at a time.

KARA POWELL
EXECUTIVE DIRECTOR, FULLER YOUTH INSTITUTE

ENDORSEMENTS

The first step in reaching the next generation is building a team that places high value on the next generation. "It's Just A Phase" is one of the best resources to keep that team on the same page fighting for the hearts of kids and teenagers. Every staff should make this required reading.

MARK BATTERSON
NEW YORK TIMES BEST SELLING AUTHOR
LEAD PASTOR, NATIONAL COMMUNITY CHURCH

Parents and church leaders both usually overestimate the time they have and underestimate their influence. You will love how this book helps you, as a leader or a parent, leverage both time and influence at every stage of the adventure.

CAREY NIEUWHOF
LEAD PASTOR, CONNEXUS

TABLE OF CONTENTS

PHASE

A TIMEFRAME

IN A **KID'S LIFE** WHEN YOU CAN

LEVERAGE

DISTINCTIVE | OPPORTUNITIES | TO | INFLUENCE

THEIR **FUTURE.**

The average educator will spend over 5,000 hours studying
child development before they try to teach a class.
That's a lot of homework.

A typical pediatrician will spend ten years and nearly half a million
dollars so they can practice medicine with children.
That's a big investment.

The manufacturer of the top-selling toy, Barbie, will spend an estimated
$600,000,000 a year to win the heart of a typical eight-year-old girl.
That's a lot of ads.

The point is sometimes it takes a lot of time, effort, and investment if you want to have influence with kids.

It's true for . . .
teachers who want to help kids learn.
doctors who want to help kids heal.
toy makers who want to help kids play.

And it's also true for any church that wants to help kids grow in their relationship with God.

You have to make an ongoing investment learning *about* kids
if you hope to have consistent influence *with* kids.

That's why "It's Just a Phase" is not just this one book.
These pages are not designed to be everything you need or want to know.
This is not intended to be a final authoritative resource,
but actually just the beginning of a continuing conversation.

This project includes hundreds of hours of research and interviews.
We've met with over a dozen licensed professional counselors,
surveyed 250 state teachers of the year,
dialogued with hundreds of age-group ministry staff,
and collaborated with 13 national leaders and authors with countless hours
of combined experience working with age-group ministries.

The result? A myriad of resources, including a series of short guides
for parents and small group leaders, digital training tools, video elements, and graphic summaries.

"It's Just a Phase" is not the effort of one or two people,
but over 50
discussing and debating for over 30 months
reading more than a hundred books and periodicals
to learn everything they can about how kids learn and develop.

The goal is to summarize and simplify an overwhelming amount of research related to child development so the average leader and parent can understand kids better.

A parent has 936 weeks between a child's birth and graduation. We don't want you to miss what's happening during the critical phases of growing up.

A PHASE IS DEFINED AS A TIME FRAME IN A KID'S LIFE WHEN YOU CAN LEVERAGE DISTINCTIVE OPPORTUNITIES TO INFLUENCE THEIR FUTURE.

And since the church is strategically positioned to influence those who influence kids, this book targets those who lead and work with kids and teenagers.

When it comes to children and youth ministries, a host of churches admit that too often . . .
Parents just don't get what the church is trying to do.
Staff don't get each other.
Volunteers don't get their role.
And too many kids get lost in transitions.

But when churches become intentional about understanding and leveraging what is actually happening in the stages of a kid's life, it changes how they . . .
Partner with families at pivotal transitions.
Teach comprehensively from preschool through college.
Train leaders how to work with specific age groups.
Improve dialogue and cooperation between ministries.
Resource parents to interact with kids in the home.

At the heart of this initiative is one primary concern.

Too many kids grow up and miss experiencing God's unconditional love and forgiveness.

Some miss it even though they grow up inside the church.
Others miss it because they grow up outside the church.
But we think many miss it because *we* missed something.

Maybe we missed . . .

EMBRACING them physically as toddlers
when they were yearning to know they were safe and loved.

ENGAGING their imagination as second graders
so they could discover how God's story intersected with their story.

AFFIRMING their worth as they transitioned
through puberty and middle school toward increasingly challenging questions.

MOBILIZING them to serve in high school,
so they walked away never experiencing what God can do through them.

The point is that we can't afford to miss it.

EVERY PHASE IS CRUCIAL.

Every phase has its own

.... | .... | ....

SIGNIFICANT RELATIONSHIPS | PRESENT REALITIES | DISTINCTIVE OPPORTUNITIES

.... | .... | ....

So we have to pay attention.
We have to do our homework.
We have to show up consistently.
We have to rally the church to know that kids matter at every phase.

The "Phase Profiles" on the following pages are designed to remind parents why every phase matters and to highlight at least 13 things leaders like you can do about it.

ZERO
TO
ONE

THE PHASE **WHEN** → **NOBODY SLEEPS,**

AND ONE MESMERIZING BABY ⇐ EVERYBODY SMELLS,

CONVINCES YOU, **"I NEED YOU NOW."**

THERE IS NOTHING LIKE SLEEP DEPRIVATION IN THE HOME OF NEW PARENTS.
Maybe that's why every book on babies seems to be primarily dedicated to keeping them happy (stop the crying, please!) or helping them sleep longer (so parents can sleep longer). Sleep is the most prized commodity of parents at this phase. In fact, if you're the stop-by-the-home-of-new-parents type just remember this: a sleeping baby is your cue not to stay.

IF YOU WONDER WHY EVERYBODY SMELLS, CONSIDER THIS:
When faced with the choice between sleep or a shower, there are days (no one's counting how many) when cleanliness doesn't win out. That's not to mention the dirty diapers or spit-up. The smells aren't all bad though. Just watch how long it takes grandma to lean over and sniff a new baby the first time she meets him.

THE GREATEST CHARACTERISTIC OF THIS PHASE BY FAR IS JUST HOW MUCH A BABY NEEDS YOU.
They need you more desperately, more consistently, and more frequently than at any other stage of life. They need you to feed them. They need you to clean up their messes. They need you to help them get to sleep. They need you to comfort them. They need you to smile at them, entertain them, and engage them. They're completely dependent on you in a way they never will be again. There is remarkable potential in the life of a new baby. And although the days are long, and the task can feel demanding, only one thing matters most at this phase—you show up.

936 WEEKS AND COUNTING . . .
UNTIL GRADUATION

ONE & TWO

THE PHASE **WHEN** → NOBODY'S ON TIME,

AND ONE EAGER TODDLER ⇐ EVERYTHING'S A MESS,

↓

WILL INSIST, **"I CAN DO IT."**

EXPECT FAMILIES TO BE LATE DURING THIS PHASE.
Maybe a parent had to wait for their toddler to "do it myself" (just try and stop them). Maybe someone impressively filled a clean diaper just as everyone was ready to get into the car. Or maybe someone slept late for the first time all week and everyone took advantage. This phase is destined to make even the most punctual adult miss the mark occasionally.

YOU CAN ALSO LOOK FORWARD TO A FEW FASHION STATEMENTS.
You may notice mismatched outfits, magic marker tattoos, sticker collages, and other various states of creative expression. In this phase, parents and leaders will learn to choose not only their battles, but also which messes will just have to be tolerated (or enjoyed, depending on your personality).

ONE OF THE GREATEST TENSIONS OF THIS PHASE CAN BE SUMMED UP IN THE PHRASE "I CAN DO IT."
Some toddlers insist more strongly than others. Some throw tantrums with greater theatrics if you try to help. This is when the struggle for independence begins to kick in. You feel it the first time they try to feed themselves and dump applesauce down the front of their shirt. In this quest for independence, three things are true: They will make mistakes. They will move too slowly. There will be a mess. Remember, they are not only learning new skills, they are also developing the confidence they need in order to move on to the next phase.

884 WEEKS AND COUNTING . . .

THREE & FOUR

THE PHASE **WHEN** →

ANYTHING CAN BE **IMAGINED,**

AND ONE CURIOUS PRESCHOOLER

← EVERYTHING CAN BE A GAME,

WANTS TO KNOW,

"WHY?"

IN THIS PHASE, THERE IS NO DISTINCTION BETWEEN IMAGINATION AND REALITY.
They might have imaginary friends or become self-proclaimed princesses, pirates, or superheroes. You might walk into a room to discover it's really a train station, a castle, an exotic island, or all three. While that's delightful at times, the imaginary may also turn scary. Fear may set in when at any given moment a monster can show up in the hallway, a snake can be under the bed, or a dragon can walk through the living room.

ONE OF THE BEST THINGS ABOUT THIS AGE IS EVERYTHING CAN BE A GAME.
You can easily get them excited about cleaning up their room if you just turn it into a game. You can make learning irresistible when you take the time to make it fun. When you're having fun, they'll have fun with you. And there may simply be nothing more entertaining than the spontaneous laughter of a three-year-old.

THEIR NEWFOUND CURIOSITY MAY BECOME A LITTLE EXHAUSTING.
Spending time with this phase may seem like a visit to your therapist or an investigative reporter: "Why?" "Why?" "Why?" But when a four-year-old asks why, they aren't looking for a deep philosophical answer. They just want to know how things are happening. When they ask why the second and third times, they aren't doubting the truth of your answer. They're just looking for more of the wonderful knowledge they know you must have as an adult person.

780 WEEKS AND COUNTING . . .

KINDERGARTEN & FIRST

THE PHASE **WHEN** → UNFILTERED WORDS MAKE YOU LAUGH,

AND LIFE BECOMES A STAGE ← HOMEWORK MAKES YOU CRY,

WHERE YOUR KID SHOUTS, **"LOOK AT ME."**

THIS PHASE IS FULL OF PERSONALITY AND MEMORABLE STATEMENTS.

By this age, a child can talk in sentences . . . and long run-on sentences, paragraphs, and wandering monologues. Sometimes it may seem as if the only goal for conversation is to Just-Keep-Talking. You will be amazed and entertained by all the profound and uncensored things they say. "I'm half Irish and half human." "How did you get the wrinkles out of your hair?" "When I grow up, I'm going to have bracelets on my teeth." "You're talking so much I can't hear you."

AMID ALL THIS DELIGHTFUL EXCHANGE, THERE IS ONE MAJOR CULTURAL SHIFT—SCHOOL.

This means less time for play, more early morning alarm clocks, and a higher demand for focused attention. While kids at this age thrive on routine and predictability, they also crave opportunities to have a little unstructured play, a chance to skip and run, to throw and catch, and to use their imagination.

WHEN FORMAL EDUCATION STARTS, SO DOES COMPETITION FOR ADULT ATTENTION.

Where previously a kid might have been one adorable toddler drawing the attention of multiple adults, they are now in a classroom with multiple kids—some even as cute and as smart as they are. At school, at church, or on the soccer field, one thing is true: the moment you show up, they will start talking to you if they are the only one there. They want your undivided attention. They want your focus. They want your approval. So give it, as freely and as often as you can to as many as possible.

676 WEEKS AND COUNTING . . .

SECOND & THIRD

THE PHASE **WHEN** →

FAIRNESS MATTERS MOST,

AND YOUR ENTHUSIASTIC KID

← DIFFERENCES GET NOTICED,

THINKS ANYTHING

"SOUNDS LIKE FUN!"

THESE CONCRETE THINKERS ARE PRIME FOR ENFORCING THE LAW IN EVERY SITUATION.

Rules are rules. Gifts should be distributed equally. Consequences should be consistent. But now your loving child has become the heat: CSI, Nancy Drew, Barney Fife. Whatever their badge, should you deviate from these guidelines to, say, surprise one kid with a treat not given to the rest, you will find yourself quickly apprehended and convicted for offenses of unfairness.

EVEN THOUGH LIFE SHOULD BE FAIR, IT'S OKAY THAT PEOPLE ARE DIFFERENT.

As second and third graders settle into formal education, they begin to notice (yes, even for the first time) that "not everyone is like me." Until now, everyone was on equal footing. Seriously, what Kindergartner isn't "the best" at everything? By second grade, kids take notice of qualities that make one kid athletic and another artistic, one kid blond and another brown-skinned. Expect a new world of adjectives in this phase as kids begin to tell you more about their growing social world.

KIDS IN THIS PHASE ARE A BEAUTIFUL BLEND OF CAPABLE AND DEPENDENT.

It's the golden age of childhood. No one should have a favorite phase—especially since life should be fair—but if you like this phase *a whole lot*, you aren't alone. Kids aren't especially needy; some might even begin to stay home alone for a couple hours without a babysitter. But they are still kids. Impressionable, enthusiastic, eager, and excited about what you are excited about. You still set the schedule, and if you think something sounds like fun you can convince them that it really is fun.

572 WEEKS AND COUNTING . . .

FOURTH & FIFTH

THE PHASE **WHEN** → **FRIENDS ARE BEST FRIENDS,**

AND YOUR CONFIDENT KID ← GAMES ARE FOR COMPETITION,

WILL INSIST, **"I'VE GOT THIS."**

IN THIS PHASE FRIENDS MATTER A LOT MORE.

Call it a club. Call it a clique. Call it a team. A tribe mentality begins to form during fourth and fifth grade. Some friends will become "best friends" and some other kids won't get invited to the party. If you see a fourth or fifth grader doing, saying, or wearing something that confuses you, check out what their peers are doing, saying or wearing. Peer approval (and disapproval) is significantly motivating in this phase. Don't worry, your opinion will matter again . . . in maybe another ten years.

IF YOU WANT TO GET THEIR ATTENTION, MAKE IT A COMPETITION.

With a "lifetime" of experience under-their-belt and a "no fear" attitude, a kid in this phase is virtually unstoppable. They are ready to prove themselves, ready for the world to take notice, and they lack the self-consciousness that might otherwise hold them back or slow them down. They can't wait to show you just how smart and fast and strong they really are.

THIS IS THE TOP OF THE ELEMENTARY SCHOOL FOOD CHAIN.

Everybody's morals are roughly aligned and their life experience is still limited enough that everything makes sense. Maybe that's why this phase usually demonstrates a clarity of mind that comes with knowing the ropes and feeling knowledgeable about what makes the world tick. Lean into that confidence and build it. Let them know you see their potential and you believe in it. There's no such thing as an overly confident middle schooler.

468 WEEKS AND COUNTING . . .

SIXTH

THE PHASE **WHEN** →

THERE'S NEVER ENOUGH **GROCERIES,**

AND A DRAMATIC KID THAT NEEDS SOMEONE ←

TOO MANY HORMONES

↓

TO PROVE,

"WHO CARES."

NO PHASE HAS LESS CONSISTENCY THAN SIXTH GRADE.
Some sixth graders still sleep with stuffed animals and some want to sleep with their new cell phone. Most sixth graders are alternately one and then the other on any given day—or any given hour. They may appear sloppy and unkempt one moment and preppy and overdressed the next. That's what makes every day a new day to discover who this growing person really is.

IN THESE 52 WEEKS, A KID MAY GROW THREE INCHES AND GAIN TEN POUNDS.
But the place you're most likely to notice the growth is in your grocery bill. Keep the pantry stocked. If you are leading sixth graders, bring french fries. Ultimate mic drop. Win.

DURING THIS YEAR, THERE WILL BE TEARS (BOTH YOURS AND THEIRS).
Doors will slam. Drama will happen. Hormones will soar. Friends will break up. Abnormal has become the norm. But amid all the ups and downs, in these changing tides of emotions, now is the time to lean in even more closely.
When they push, prove you can't be pushed away.
When they change, prove you will love them consistently.
When they break your trust, prove you are someone who can be trusted.
It may seem challenging, but keep up the chase so in this phase there's never any reason to wonder, "Who cares?"

364 WEEKS AND COUNTING . . .

SEVENTH & EIGHTH

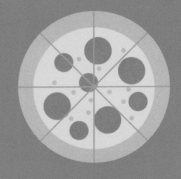

THE PHASE **WHEN** →

NOTHING YOU DO **IS COOL,**

AND ONE SMART KID

← EVERYTHING IS FUN IN A CROWD,

WILL KEEP REMINDING YOU,

"YEAH . . . I KNOW."

NOW YOU WILL BEGIN TO REALIZE JUST HOW EMBARRASSING YOU CAN BE.
Figuring out the new rules for your social behavior can be intimidating. When is it acceptable to "like" their Instagram post, and when are you allowed to openly comment? When are you expected to show up to the game, and whose parents are you not supposed to talk to? When are you supposed to dress up and be impressive, and when are you supposed to just be casual?

INSECURITY IS AN UNSPOKEN FORCE THAT KEEPS THIS PHASE WONDERFULLY AWKWARD.
Even the most confident seventh grader may choose a "group" Halloween costume. ("Let's go together as rock, paper, scissors!") They walk the hall in pairs. They go to the mall with a herd. They build unfathomably large social media platforms. The name of the game is to never be caught alone and to always associate with the coolest crowd possible.

YOU MAY BE SURPRISED AT HOW SMART KIDS IN THIS PHASE REALLY ARE.
In fact, there may be no phase quite as smart as this one—just ask them. Being so much smarter than everyone else can really become a burden. Sometimes the patience just runs out, and they simply can't explain it to you one more time. The important thing will be what they know, and how they begin to personalize it in this phase. So look for ways to encourage their process (just remember that it's *their* process and they know it).

312 WEEKS AND COUNTING . . .

NINTH

THE PHASE **WHEN** → FRIENDSHIPS SHIFT, **GRADES COUNT,**

YOUR TEENAGER ← AND INTERESTS CHANGE SO OFTEN

HAS TO EXPLAIN

"THIS IS ME NOW."

YOU MAY NOTICE FORMER BEST FRIENDS FADING AND NEW FRIENDS APPEARING.

The average high school has 750 teenagers, 250 dating couples, and more than 50 options for extracurricular activities. With so many opportunities to connect, it's no wonder teenagers in this phase abandon the general quest for popularity and search for acceptance in more specialized groups. A teenager may find their place in shop class or on the debate team, in drama club or on the baseball field, in Future Farmers of America or Beta Club.

THESE 52 WEEKS ALSO BRING A NEW ACADEMIC REALITY.

The demand for personal responsibility increases and teens are held to more rigorous standards. For some, this is when grades begin to count toward admission to the exclusive and elusive college of their dreams. Even if a selective college isn't obviously in the cards, grades still count toward a high school diploma, and sometimes toward extra privileges at home. No matter what, for every ninth grader, grades count.

THIS IS A YEAR OF IDENTIFYING TALENTS AND ABILITIES.

Freshmen gravitate to where they are most accepted. By the end of this year, your teenager will likely have a more stable sense of who they are than they have for the past three years. Frankly, they may be a little frustrated that you haven't known who they were all along. (Why not? It's been so obvious.) Listen carefully. Pay attention. Stalk them openly. The greatest thing you can do in this phase is to know them and know where they are finding acceptance. Perhaps nothing will affect the trajectory of the next four years more.

208 WEEKS AND COUNTING . . .

TENTH

THE PHASE **WHEN** → "EVERYONE ELSE **CAN . . . , "**

AND YOUR RESOLUTE TEEN ← "NOBODY ELSE HAS TO . . . ,"

WILL PUSH YOU TO ANSWER, **"WHY NOT?"**

THIS PHASE MARKS A YEAR OF INDEPENDENCE.

Sweet Sixteen means sweet freedom. Whether this is getting a driver's license or having friends who have one, there is a deliverance from authority when a teenager no longer depends on Mom or Dad for transportation. Just how much freedom they should have, and just how much freedom their peers have, you will never really know. If you ask them, no other adult on the planet limits the activities as much as you.

SOPHOMORE YEAR IS A BLEND OF FRESH SKEPTICISM AND NEW DISCOVERIES.

With newfound freedom comes greater life experience. Whatever a tenth grader believed in theory has now been tested. That really life-shattering bad thing you warned them about? They know someone who survived it. The standards you held up for them in the past? They realize you haven't always lived by them. Get ready for them to challenge the process.

THE DAYS OF "BECAUSE I SAID SO" ARE FAR BEHIND YOU.

A sophomore still needs boundaries, but unless the boundary makes sense in light of their personal (and changing) beliefs, they won't stay within it. You're probably the same way. Unlike you, however, a sophomore doesn't have your past experience or your future orientation. So when you "debate" (loudly) boundaries with a sophomore, remember to stay in the present. They aren't challenging what you both want ten years from now, they just need you to understand what they need *right now*.

156 WEEKS AND COUNTING . . .

ELEVENTH

THE PHASE **WHEN** → THERE'S LESS **DRAMA,**

AND YOUR VERY BUSY TEENAGER ← **MORE STRESS**

ANSWERS ALL YOUR QUESTIONS WITH

"JUST TRUST ME."

JUNIORS ARE MORE READY THAN EVER TO BE WHO THEY REALLY ARE.

The rapid influx of hormones has regulated, the fight for peer acceptance has subsided, and the intensity of conflict over independence . . . well, they've worn you down. This confidence is enough to let you relax emotionally, and allow yourself to be amazed at all they can accomplish.

"ACCOMPLISH" IS THE BEST WORD TO DESCRIBE THE ACTIVITY IN THIS PHASE.

Many must pass an end-of-year graduation test to receive a high school diploma. Some may also begin an after-school job. Many juniors focus on building a college resume by adding a growing number of AP courses, an internship, volunteer activities, extracurricular leadership roles and SAT prep. For a select few, it's when recruitment for college sports begins. Whether your teen is caught up in the race to win or simply trying to survive, junior year easily has the highest pressure.

WITH ALL THAT'S HAPPENING, DON'T BE SURPRISED IF IT'S HARD TO KEEP UP.

"Where are you going?" "Who are you going with?" "When will you be back?" "How long have you been dating?" Your relationship may begin to feel a little one-sided. It's okay. They don't expect you to keep up. What they really want is for you to trust them. After all, they will be out of the house soon and you will have to anyway. Let this be a practice year for both of you. Help them prove the ways they can be trusted, choose your battles wisely and parent them in the areas that seem to be most challenging for them personally.

104 WEEKS AND COUNTING . . .

TWELFTH

THE PHASE WHEN → **YOUR EMERGING ADULT PULLS AWAY, GETS CLOSER,**

AND YOU BOTH ← **DOES THINGS FOR THE LAST TIME**

START ASKING, **"WHAT'S NEXT?"**

IF SIXTEEN IS "SWEET," THEN EIGHTEEN IS "LEGAL."

This kid is no longer a child. Technically speaking, they are fully responsible for their actions and decisions. (Of course, you may still have to pick up the pieces from time to time.) You may feel them pull away as they drive to a first job, deposit a paycheck, register to vote, or maybe even disengage from youth ministry programs.

THE COUNTDOWN CLOCK IS COUNTING DOWN TO THE END.

There may seem to be an urgency to these last 52 weeks. As a senior takes on more responsibility, they will also lean in relationally in a different way. They discover—especially late in the year—that they need the adults in their world a little bit more than they thought. All of a sudden the decisions have very high stakes. Like, "Will you try to date him long-distance?" And there's nothing like having "last time" moments to bring out a little sentimentality.

THE GREATEST QUESTION OF THIS PHASE FOR EVERYONE IS, "WHAT'S NEXT?"

In fact, it can drive you both a little crazy. At times it can feel like walking on a moving sidewalk that's about to end with no real defined floor to walk onto. Just remember to focus on "next: few months" more than "next: rest-of-your-life." They may be legally adults, but they aren't adults *really*. Your job hasn't ended. Even the most accomplished seniors will take a few years (and maybe some counseling) to figure this adult thing out.

52 WEEKS AND COUNTING . . .

EIGHTEEN +

THE PHASE **WHEN**  YOUR EMERGING ADULT **PULLS AWAY MORE, NEEDS YOU AGAIN,** DOES THINGS FOR THE FIRST TIME

AND YOU BOTH

KEEP ASKING, **"WHAT NOW?"**

THIS IS THE YEAR YOU HAVE IMAGINED FOR EIGHTEEN YEARS.

You may be surprised how loud the emptiness sounds when someone who has been familiar in your world suddenly disappears. Of course, you may also rediscover a little personal freedom of your own. What do you mean there's no game to attend, no form to sign, no forgotten books to take to the school at the last minute? And how did we not finish the milk before it expired?

THEY MAY COST YOU MORE EVEN THOUGH YOU SEE THEM LESS.

Even if they aren't physically present, their presence may still be felt—especially in your bank account. Whether you are helping fund their continued education or making a deposit for their first apartment, there's a good chance you haven't stopped paying for some expenses in their world. They may also cost you some unpredictable time as well. You never know when they may call looking for advice, affirmation, or maybe just a reminder of home.

GIVE ADVICE WHEN THEY ASK FOR IT.

The good news is that every 18 and 19-year-old knows what they want and has a precise plan for their life. Wait? That's not true? They might amaze you with all they can do on their own, but there's also still a lot left to figure out. Where will they live? Will they get married? What kind of work will ultimately bring them fulfillment? They want your advice, but only in small doses, and only when they ask for it. This is a season to re-engage your child in a new way, not as a parent but more as a peer as you transition your relationship for the future.

STILL COUNTING . . .

The following diagram will not make any sense until you read the book. But a really smart leader suggested we put it at the beginning of the book to provide a reference for what you are about to read. Kind of like the map of Middle Earth that Tolkien put in the front of *Lord of the Rings*. Sometimes it helps to see the big picture before you read the parts so you can see how everything fits together. We also put this diagram at the end. We really don't want you to miss it.

PHASE
TIMELINE
OVERVIEW

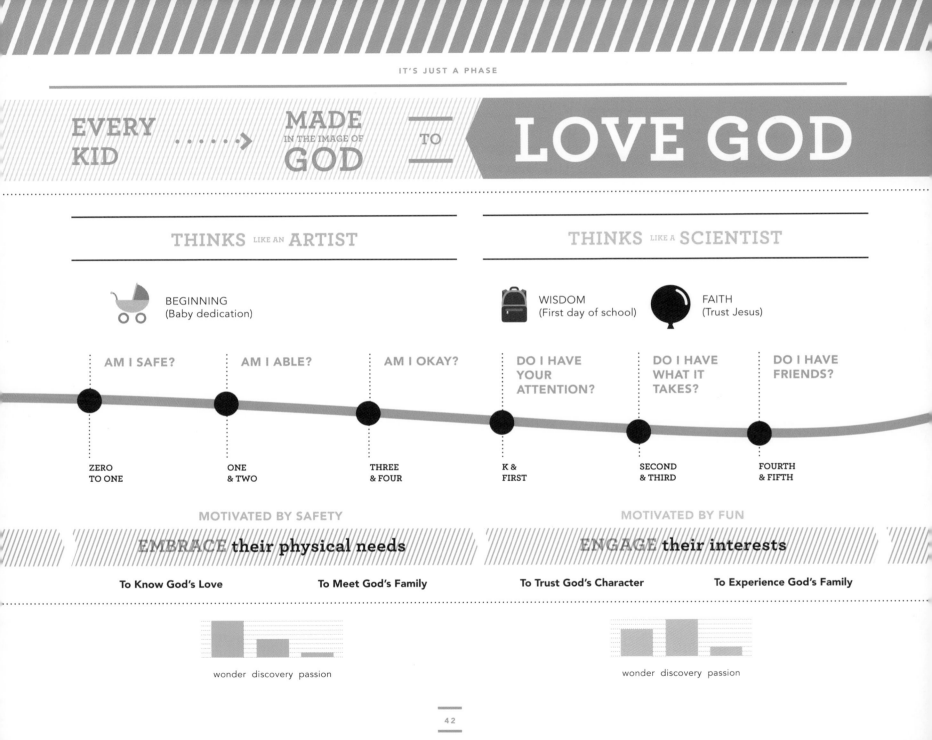

EVERY KID ·····> MADE IN THE IMAGE OF GOD ⎯TO⎯ # LOVE GOD

THINKS LIKE AN ARTIST

THINKS LIKE A SCIENTIST

BEGINNING
(Baby dedication)

WISDOM
(First day of school)

FAITH
(Trust Jesus)

AM I SAFE?

AM I ABLE?

AM I OKAY?

DO I HAVE YOUR ATTENTION?

DO I HAVE WHAT IT TAKES?

DO I HAVE FRIENDS?

ZERO TO ONE

ONE & TWO

THREE & FOUR

K & FIRST

SECOND & THIRD

FOURTH & FIFTH

MOTIVATED BY SAFETY

MOTIVATED BY FUN

EMBRACE their physical needs

ENGAGE their interests

To Know God's Love

To Meet God's Family

To Trust God's Character

To Experience God's Family

wonder discovery passion

wonder discovery passion

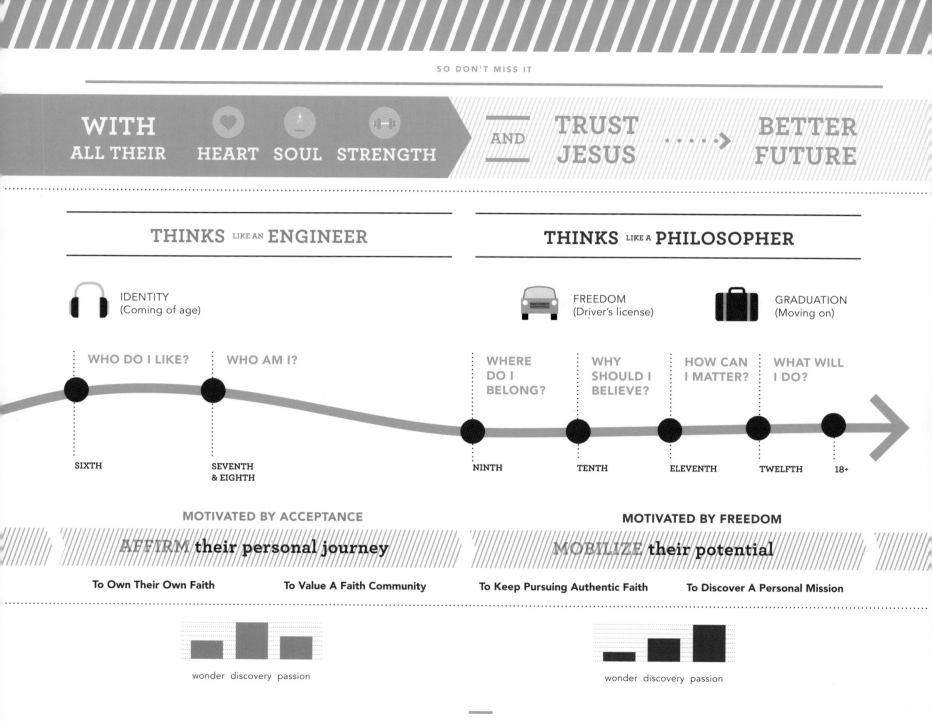

WITH ALL THEIR **HEART** **SOUL** **STRENGTH** AND TRUST JESUS · · · · > BETTER FUTURE

THINKS LIKE AN ENGINEER

THINKS LIKE A PHILOSOPHER

IDENTITY
(Coming of age)

FREEDOM
(Driver's license)

GRADUATION
(Moving on)

WHO DO I LIKE?

WHO AM I?

WHERE DO I BELONG?

WHY SHOULD I BELIEVE?

HOW CAN I MATTER?

WHAT WILL I DO?

SIXTH

SEVENTH & EIGHTH

NINTH

TENTH

ELEVENTH

TWELFTH

18+

MOTIVATED BY ACCEPTANCE

MOTIVATED BY FREEDOM

AFFIRM *their personal journey*

MOBILIZE *their potential*

To Own Their Own Faith   To Value A Faith Community

To Keep Pursuing Authentic Faith   To Discover A Personal Mission

wonder discovery passion

wonder discovery passion

EVERY PHASE HAS

SIGNIFICANT RELATIONSHIPS

TO INFLUENCE

SO

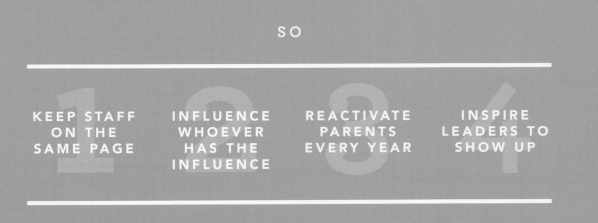

KEEP STAFF ON THE SAME PAGE

INFLUENCE WHOEVER HAS THE INFLUENCE

REACTIVATE PARENTS EVERY YEAR

INSPIRE LEADERS TO SHOW UP

That includes ...
parents
small group leaders
decision makers
first cousins
and senior pastors.

If you gain influence in a kid's life now,
you stand a better chance of having
influence with them later
when it matters even more.

That's why every phase of a kid's
life gives your church
a new opportunity to connect kids
to a significant relationship.

Remember, churches are not really losing influence
with an entire generation.

They are actually losing influence with a lot of

Individual Families
Individual Parents
Individual Kids

So don't miss it.
Influence someone
who will influence
a kid at every phase.

KEEP STAFF ON THE SAME PAGE

SO KIDS AT EVERY PHASE WILL BE CONNECTED TO A MASTER PLAN

Now that you have read a quick description of each phase,
here's a complicated question.

WHICH PHASE OF A KID'S LIFE DO YOU THINK IS MOST IMPORTANT?

There are actually two answers to that question.

ANSWER 1.

THE PHASE THAT SHOULD MATTER MOST IS THE ONE YOU ARE WORKING WITH NOW.

In other words, you should learn to champion the age group you work with so you can become a specialist. That's why churches need age-group pastors or directors. Specialists provide focus, and focus gives a ministry momentum and relevance. The difference between a stagnant swamp and a flowing river is focus and power. Which one do you want to characterize your ministry?

A specialist stays focused on what a kid needs now.

ANSWER 2.

THE PHASE THAT MATTERS MOST HAPPENS BEFORE AND AFTER THIS PHASE.

Hopefully that sounds confusing. Why? Effective ministries know how to focus on a specific age group and see the overall vision for a kid's life. That means as an age-group leader you need to develop the skill to be a specialist and a generalist, simultaneously.

A generalist owns the vision for where a kid is going.

Specialists will champion a few phases. Generalists will champion every phase.

It's okay to be 80 percent specialist and 20 percent generalist, as long as you know how to take off the specialist hat occasionally and think like a generalist. Thinking like a generalist prevents your ministry from becoming an island. It also forces you to think about the master plan so a kid keeps moving in the right direction.

Just remember:
Some leaders are better at being generalists.
Some leaders are better at being specialists.
But every leader needs to get better at both.

GENERALISTS

SPECIALISTS

GENERALISTS SEE THE FOREST	SPECIALISTS SEE THE TREES
GENERALISTS SEE THE SIMILARITIES	SPECIALISTS SEE THE DISTINCTIVES
GENERALISTS SEE THE CONNECTIONS	SPECIALISTS SEE THE SEPARATIONS

When your staff members start thinking like specialists and generalists, everyone begins to see each other's ministry in a different light. They make fewer wrong assumptions about each other's age group programs.
They won't ask . . .
Why do preschool leaders just sing silly, rhyming songs?
Why do middle school leaders play stupid, gross games?
Why do high school leaders . . . wait, why can't we find the high school leaders?

When you're on the same page as a staff, it's easier to get other significant relationships like parents and volunteers on the same page.

When everyone is on the same page it . . .
magnifies your focus,
synchronizes your efforts,
and increases your momentum.

When you wear the hat of a specialist and a generalist . . .
respect between age group ministries goes up.
families know how to cooperate with your strategy.
staff value meeting and collaboration.
kids transition between age groups effectively.
you develop a common language that connects everyone.

You can actually start speaking a common language immediately. Here are four words that can connect every parent, staff, and volunteer to everything they need to know about phases. (How is that for oversimplifying?)

Just remember:

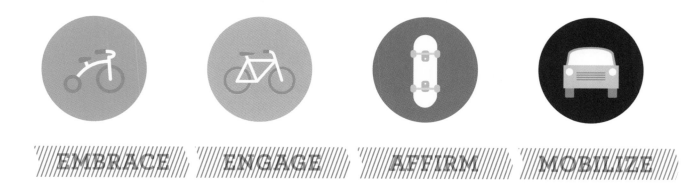

EMBRACE   ENGAGE   AFFIRM   MOBILIZE

These words will grow in meaning over the next few chapters.

INFLUENCE WHOEVER HAS THE INFLUENCE

2

SO KIDS AT EVERY PHASE WILL HAVE A CHAMPION WHO MAKES THEM A PRIORITY

If you're reading this book, more than likely it's because
you influence children or teenagers.

That puts you in a unique tribe of leaders who spend every week
teaching, programming, and leading the next generation.

It also means it's up to you.

You are in a position to change how . . .
adults in your church see kids and teenagers.
nonbelieving parents see your church.
Christian families see their neighbors.
lead pastors see children and youth ministry.
volunteers see what they do every week.

You have a list of influencers to influence. And surely you have realized by now
that all of the people on that list are adults—not kids.

The only way to change the priorities of adults is to make adults your priority.
When you learn how to influence influencers effectively, two things happen:
Influencers who don't care start caring.
Influencers who care start caring even more.

Every children's pastor and student pastor lives
by this simple code for success:

YOU CAN'T CHAMPION A BETTER FUTURE FOR KIDS
UNLESS YOU CONSISTENTLY CHALLENGE THE PRIORITIES OF ADULTS.

That's why you have to convince someone that . . .

what happens in a fourth grade small group
is just as important as what happens in "Big Church."

there needs to be a line item in the budget for
goldfish crackers, glitter, and beach balls.

the lead pastor needs to preach a
Sunday-morning series on why family matters.

the same volunteers need
to show up every week.

what happens at home
is more important than what happens at church.

"EVERY CHILD DESERVES A CHAMPION, AN ADULT WHO WILL NEVER GIVE UP ON THEM, WHO UNDERSTANDS THE POWER OF CONNECTION, AND INSISTS THAT THEY BECOME THE BEST THAT THEY CAN POSSIBLY BE."

RITA PIERSON

LIFELONG EDUCATOR

You have to remind everyone . . .

IT'S NOT BABYSITTING.	IT'S DISCIPLESHIP.
IT'S NOT PIZZA.	IT'S A RELATIONSHIP.
IT'S NOT A PARTY.	IT'S A PLATFORM.
IT'S NOT FILLING A VOLUNTEER SLOT.	IT'S INFLUENCING SOMEONE'S FUTURE.

You have to rally every adult who has influence
to believe that kids should be a priority at every phase.

That's what champions do.
They reason, persuade, challenge, beg, manipulate, and inspire
someone to do whatever needs to be done
for the sake of a kid's future.

Champions get up every morning of every week
thinking about how they can lead better.

Champions have to lead in every direction at the same time.
You have to lead up and down. And you have to lead out and in.
     Up — to get the lead pastor to sign off.
 Down — to get the volunteer to show up.
   Out — to get the staff to go along.
     In — to get your heart in the right place.

CHAMPIONS HAVE TO LEAD IN EVERY DIRECTION AT THE SAME TIME

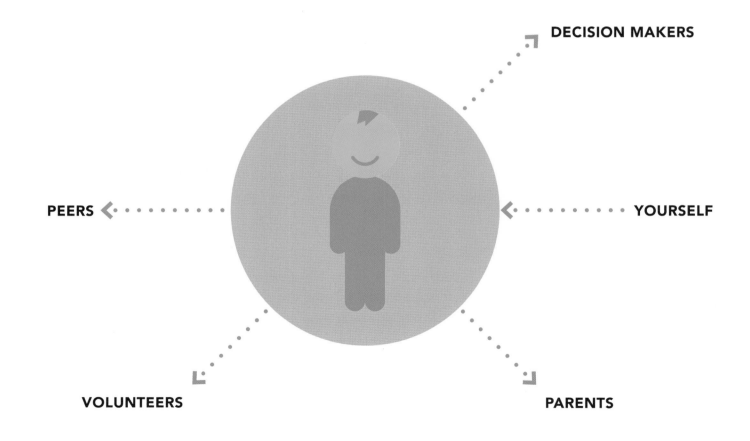

DECISION MAKERS

PEERS

YOURSELF

VOLUNTEERS

PARENTS

If you are going to champion a ministry for kids or teenagers, here are some questions you need ask yourself every Monday morning.

AM I COMMUNICATING THE STRATEGY CLEARLY?

Champions have to communicate, and their words matter immensely. Over time, words create a common language to keep everyone motivated and aligned. But words should be more than inspiring. They should also be insightful and strategic. Even a single word can make an impact. This book was designed to provide a common language to help age group leaders stay focused. Imagine if every leader knew that when they . . .

EMBRACE preschoolers physically, it gives a first impression of a heavenly Father.

ENGAGE the interests of children, it provokes knowing God personally.

AFFIRM a middle schooler's identity, it gives a safe place to process doubts.

MOBILIZE a teenager's potential, it develops a personal vision for their future.

AM I CHALLENGING THE PROCESS RESPECTFULLY?

Champions of kids need to be avid learners. It is essential to know the changes that are happening to kids so your message and ministry stay relevant. What works this year may not be as effective next year. That's why you should read more than your Bible if you care what kids think about the Bible. Be sure to do your homework before you show up to make your case in front of volunteers, leaders, or parents. You will not always be right, but you should always be responsible. Stay as educated and informed as you possibly can. You also need to ask for a seat at the table. It doesn't even have to be your seat. Just make sure there is a seat in the decision-making circles for someone who will champion every kid at every phase.

AM I CONFRONTING THE PROBLEMS COURAGEOUSLY?

Champions have difficult conversations. It's impossible to champion a cause without frustrating a few people.
Always remember you can't move a boat through the water without making a few waves.
There will be people who don't care enough,
and you will have to move them until they care more.
There will be people who care about the wrong things,
and you may have to move them to care about what really matters.
There will be people who really only care about themselves,
and you may just have to move them out.

That doesn't mean you should be rude or insensitive or heartless. It just means you should be stubborn about making kids the priority. There will be times in your ministry when what is best for a kid may be hard for an adult. But your primary responsibility is every kid at every phase. So never put the ego of an adult over the heart of a kid.

AM I CARING FOR THE VOLUNTEERS CONSISTENTLY?

Champions always go to the front lines. You can't expect others to do what you are not willing to do. If you expect leaders to serve kids, then you need to serve leaders. If you want kids at every phase to be a priority, then their leaders have to be your priority. Specifically, that means if leaders are expected to show up weekly in the lives of children and teenagers, then you need to show up weekly in the lives of leaders. So serving leaders means you have scheduled time to connect, equip, encourage, and train your leaders this week.

3

REACTIVATE PARENTS EVERY YEAR

SO KIDS AT EVERY PHASE WILL STAY CONNECTED TO THEIR PARENTS

Regardless of how much a church learns about life stages, parents know things no one else knows about their own children. That's why parents have an advantage the church will never have related to the future of a child. A parent has history.

Just remember,
no scientist
or theorist
or expert can really know a child
the way their own parent does.

The problem with any research on child development, including what you're reading now, is that it oversimplifies and generalizes age-group characteristics. But parents know their child's patterns, tendencies, preferences, and behaviors better than anyone.

That being said, churches know something parents don't know. Churches work with multiple kids in the same phase every week. That means churches can help parents understand general characteristics of a phase so they can readjust their parenting skills.

Parenting a preschooler takes different skills than parenting a middle schooler.
(Although there are awkward conversations and smells in both.)

And kids will grow up and eventually move out one day.
(That almost always happens.)

At some point every kid will own their own
Faith
Values
Decisions
Relationships
and Future.

But if parents don't reinvent themselves, they may miss out on having the right kind
of long-term relational influence.
(Kind of like Kodak did when they ignored the digital phase.)

The point is kids are changing fast, and it's more important for
parents to stay connected than anyone.

KODAK

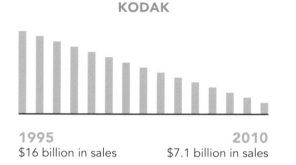

1995
$16 billion in sales

2010
$7.1 billion in sales

BLOCKBUSTER

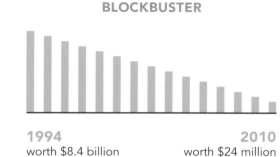

1994
worth $8.4 billion

2010
worth $24 million

IF PARENTS DON'T REINVENT HOW THEY PARENT, THEY MAY MISS OUT ON HAVING THE RIGHT KIND OF RELATIONAL INFLUENCE

DISNEY WORLD

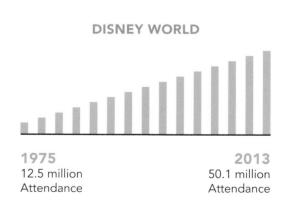

1975
12.5 million
Attendance

2013
50.1 million
Attendance

AMAZON

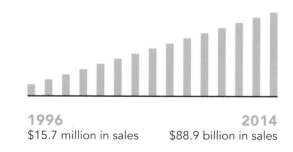

1996
$15.7 million in sales

2014
$88.9 billion in sales

Parents start out with low relational influence and high positional influence. Which is just another way of saying they are in charge of a mini-human who poops ten times a day but has extraordinary potential. So every parent has one primary goal:

Rely less on their positional influence,
and increase their relational influence
until a child can live independently.

Every parent wrestles with how to create boundaries without forfeiting the relationship with their kids. It takes a lot of practice knowing when to hold on and when to let go. Unfortunately as they practice, the amount of hours a parent has to invest in their kids relationally reduces drastically with every passing stage:

12	6	4	2
hours a day with a preschooler	hours a day with an elementary kid	hours a day with a middle schooler	hours a day with a high schooler

The window of opportunity closes fast. Each phase has an estimated number of weeks left until the average kid leaves home. These weeks are an important reminder that . . .

Parents are not really raising children.
They're raising adults.

PARENTAL INFLUENCE

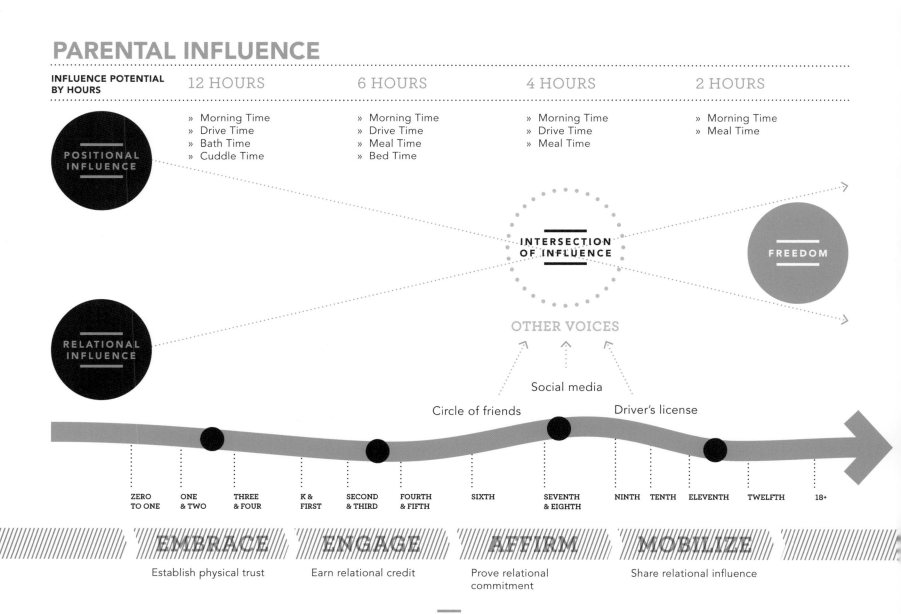

INFLUENCE POTENTIAL BY HOURS

12 HOURS	6 HOURS	4 HOURS	2 HOURS

POSITIONAL INFLUENCE

- » Morning Time
- » Drive Time
- » Bath Time
- » Cuddle Time

- » Morning Time
- » Drive Time
- » Meal Time
- » Bed Time

- » Morning Time
- » Drive Time
- » Meal Time

- » Morning Time
- » Meal Time

RELATIONAL INFLUENCE

INTERSECTION OF INFLUENCE

FREEDOM

OTHER VOICES

Social media

Circle of friends

Driver's license

| ZERO TO ONE | ONE & TWO | THREE & FOUR | K & FIRST | SECOND & THIRD | FOURTH & FIFTH | SIXTH | SEVENTH & EIGHTH | NINTH | TENTH | ELEVENTH | TWELFTH | 18+ |

EMBRACE
Establish physical trust

ENGAGE
Earn relational credit

AFFIRM
Prove relational commitment

MOBILIZE
Share relational influence

It's important to reactivate parents every year so they understand the phase of their child. It may be just a phase, but when you don't miss it, you do more than just help kids. You make sure parents don't miss it. More specifically, the most strategic thing you can do to influence the next generation is to help parents win with their own kids.

Here are a few ideas for reactivating parents:
• Create a content calendar with everything you want parents to know.
• Organize a plan to cue parents weekly with key information when they need it.
• Establish annual parent orientations to equip them for the next phase.
• Recruit leaders to connect with every parent, especially those who never show up.
• Provide resources to enhance family time in the home.

YOUR ROLE IS TO REMIND PARENTS AT EVERY PHASE TO KEEP PARENTING WITH AN END IN MIND. THINK ABOUT IT THIS WAY:

EMBRACE
THEIR PHYSICAL NEEDS

During the preschool years parents must learn to EMBRACE their child's tangible needs so they can begin to *establish physical trust.*

ENGAGE
THEIR INTERESTS

During the elementary years, parents should take a crash course in storytelling and play so they can ENGAGE the interest of their child. This will be the best time to *earn relational credit.*

AFFIRM
THEIR PERSONAL JOURNEY

During middle school, parents need to master the skill of never freaking out. This is when they learn to AFFIRM the personal journey of their tween. During this time, they will have plenty of opportunities to *prove a relational commitment.*

MOBILIZE
THEIR POTENTIAL

At ninth grade, parents start mastering the art of negotiating. They have approximately 200 weeks left to MOBILIZE their kid toward a better future. So they need to *leverage their relational influence.*

INSPIRE LEADERS TO SHOW UP

SO KIDS AT EVERY PHASE WILL HAVE A CONSISTENT VOICE BESIDES THEIR PARENT

So . . . if no volunteer can ever know what a parent knows,
then why recruit anyone to help with kids and teenagers?

It would definitely make things easier
if you could just tell parents,
"Since you know more than we can ever know,
and you have more time than we will ever have,
and you care more than we ever will,
then this is really up to you as the parent."

You could also misquote Deuteronomy 6 to convince parents it's their job alone, not the church's, to raise their kids.
Just skip the part of the text where Moses speaks to every leader in the crowd (not just parents).

MOSES WAS ACTUALLY THE FIRST GUY WITH THE IDEA, "IT TAKES A VILLAGE."

Sure, parents should be the
primary influence in their kids' lives.

But research, experts, and statistics suggest
kids who have other adults in their lives
have better odds at winning.

And what about that freaked-out mom of a middle schooler who is suddenly convinced, "Someone else is living in my kid's body, and whoever it is hates me"? (Remind her to only freak out on the inside.)

Maybe more churches should take Moses seriously when he implied, "We are all responsible for the faith and future of the kids in our community."

The more you learn about life stages,
the more you will be convinced that
kids need a consistent adult,
besides their parents.

(The phrase "consistent adult" is actually code for "weekly small group leader." Check out our book called *Lead Small Culture*.)

PRESCHOOLERS
need a consistent adult, because they can be terrified by an unfamiliar face.

ELEMENTARY KIDS
need a consistent adult, because they will tell anything to a stranger.

MIDDLE SCHOOLERS
need a consistent adult, because nothing else in their life is consistent.

HIGH SCHOOLERS
need a consistent adult, because they only trust people who show up consistently.

Every phase needs the same thing:
A CONSISTENT LEADER.

And every phase also needs something different:
A UNIQUE RESPONSE.

Some phases will . . .
cry more.
talk more.
doubt more.
do more.

That's why some leaders . . .
embrace preschoolers so they feel safe.
engage children so they can believe.
affirm middle schoolers so they will keep believing.
mobilize teenagers to participate in something significant.

**Don't be afraid to challenge leaders to make
different commitments at different phases.**

The leader who shows up once a week for second graders
will make an easy connection within a few minutes
because children will believe in anyone.

The leader who shows up for sixth graders
will have to hang out for a while.
Sixth graders are skeptics.
They need proof over time that a leader cares.

SMALL GROUP LEADER COMMITMENT

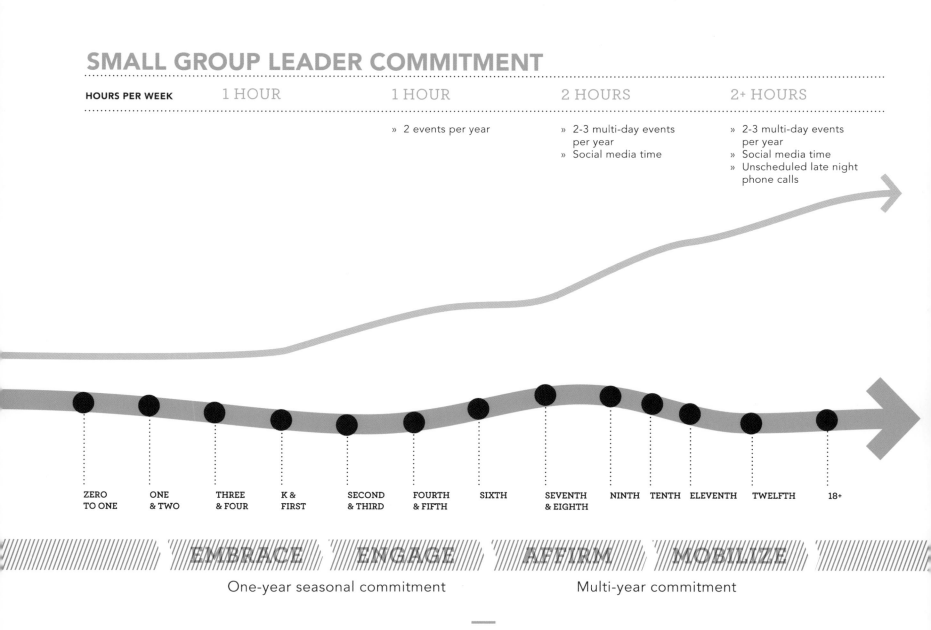

HOURS PER WEEK	1 HOUR	1 HOUR	2 HOURS	2+ HOURS
		» 2 events per year	» 2-3 multi-day events per year » Social media time	» 2-3 multi-day events per year » Social media time » Unscheduled late night phone calls

ZERO TO ONE · ONE & TWO · THREE & FOUR · K & FIRST · SECOND & THIRD · FOURTH & FIFTH · SIXTH · SEVENTH & EIGHTH · NINTH · TENTH · ELEVENTH · TWELFTH · 18+

EMBRACE · ENGAGE · AFFIRM · MOBILIZE

One-year seasonal commitment · Multi-year commitment

Yes, parents have an advantage small group leaders don't have.
They get to know one kid through multiple phases.

But a small group leader has an advantage parents don't have.
They get to know multiple kids through one phase.

That's why parents and small group leaders are both important.
Every kid needs someone who knows their history.
And every kid needs someone who can rediscover them now.

So let's start learning more about
what actually happens at every phase.

EVERY KID NEEDS A PARENT WHO HAS HISTORY **&** EVERY KID NEEDS A LEADER WHO CAN DISCOVER THEM NOW

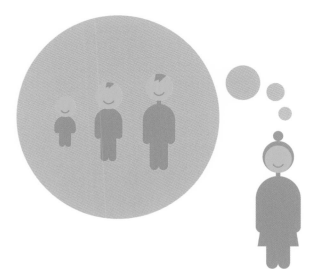

Every Parent knows their child **THROUGH MULTIPLE PHASES.**

IT'S JUST A PHASE
SO DON'T MISS IT

Every Small Group Leader knows multiple children **THROUGH ONE PHASE.**

EVERY PHASE HAS

PRESENT REALITIES

YOU NEED TO UNDERSTAND

SO

5	6	7	8
KNOW WHO THEY ARE NOW	READ THEIR MIND	DISCOVER THEIR WORLD	INTERPRET THEIR MOTIVES

Before you can lead someone where they need to go,
you need to know where they are.

That's why you need to understand what's changing
in every phase . . .
Physically
Mentally
Relationally
Culturally
Emotionally
Morally

The more you know them,
the more they will . . .
Know they matter.
Believe they can win.
Feel like they belong.
Discern what they should do.

Remember, if you don't know who you are talking to
you can't really expect them to listen.

So don't miss it.
The better you understand who kids are now,
the better they'll understand who they're meant to be.

5

KNOW WHO THEY ARE NOW

SO KIDS AT EVERY PHASE WILL KNOW THEY MATTER

Kids know more about you
than you know about them.

People are wired to pay closer attention to someone who has power over their world. Think about it. You probably know more about the President than he knows about you. As kids and teenagers grow up, they depend on the adults in their world to get food, to have transportation, and to pay for something on occasion.

It just makes sense for them to . . .
pay attention to what you like (so they can sweet-talk you later).
listen to what you dislike (so they don't accidently make you mad).
stalk your social media (so they can catch you off-guard).

Here's a relational principle for you:
You can't influence someone you don't know.

That's why marketing executives typically spend 15 percent of their budgets to simply clarify and research their target audience.

Kids and teenagers get this intuitively.
They want to have influence with you (in order to get what they want) so it's in their nature to study you. As an adult, you don't need kids the way they need you. So you have to be far more intentional about knowing them if you want to have influence.

If you are reading this book,
you care about the future of the next generation.

But if you want to *shape* their future,
they need to know they matter to you.

Lifetime educator Rita Pierson spoke at a TED Conference
to a room of educators to remind us all:
"Kids don't learn from people they don't like."

It's also true that kids don't learn from people who don't like them.
And they will never feel like you like them if you don't know them.

So, you have to know them.
What you don't know can ultimately sabotage your mission.

Like handing out antibiotics at a free clinic
but failing to leave enough medication to finish the course.

Like passing out eyeglasses to kids who can't see
without first doing an eye exam to diagnose the problem.

**Sometimes you just need to understand what you need to understand
if you want to be effective.**

"SEEK FIRST
TO UNDERSTAND,
THEN TO BE
UNDERSTOOD."

ST. FRANCIS OF ASSISI

There are two mistakes leaders tend to make when it comes to knowing kids and teenagers:

1. ADULTS TEND TO ASSUME, "THEY ARE LIKE ME NOW."
Chances are, you don't think you think this way. But if you aren't careful, you can start acting like every kid is like you. And when you act like every kid is like you, as if they have the perspective of a 22, 35, or 48-year-old, you may get discouraged.

2. ADULTS TEND TO ASSUME, "THEY ARE LIKE I USED TO BE."
After all, you were a kid once. You already survived middle school. So you know something about what it's like to grow up, right? The problem with this kind of thinking is that a lot has changed since you were a second grader (like boy bands, mobile phones, and *Frozen*).

When you assume you know what you don't know,
you risk giving kids what they don't need.

That's why you have to be careful if you're . . .
a mother of preschoolers picking music for the sixth grade lock-in or
a seminary graduate teaching two-year-olds about the crucifixion.

In the first 18+ years of a person's life, kids are changing in six fundamental ways. Those changes affect how they think, learn, feel, and relate. So, if you want to have influence, you have to understand what is changing . . .

PHYSICALLY, MENTALLY, RELATIONALLY, CULTURALLY, EMOTIONALLY, MORALLY

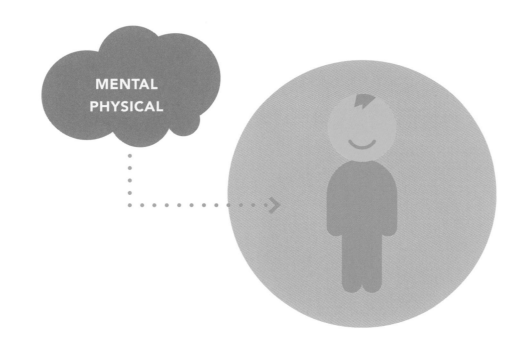

MENTAL
PHYSICAL

EVERY KID IS CHANGING PHYSICALLY AND MENTALLY

At every phase, kids are growing and developing. It's easy to see how their bodies are changing. It takes a little extra effort to chew when teeth go missing, or to walk when your legs are suddenly two inches longer than last summer. Changes also happen in a kid's brain that affect the way they think—those changes are just a lot harder to see.

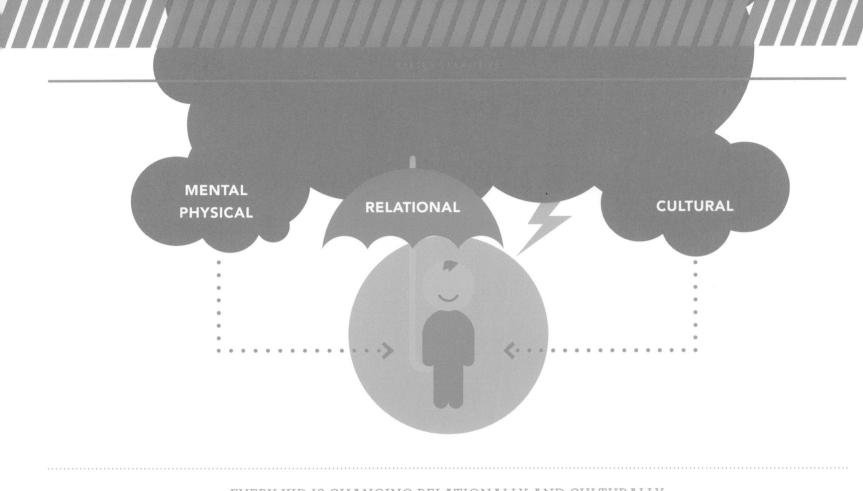

MENTAL PHYSICAL

RELATIONAL

CULTURAL

EVERY KID IS CHANGING RELATIONALLY AND CULTURALLY

At every phase, kids adjust to new challenges and develop their identity. The first cultural change happens when a baby enters the world for the first time. Talk about culture shock! At every phase cultural changes collide with mental and physical changes to create tension. How that tension is resolved relationally can empower or undermine a kid's future.

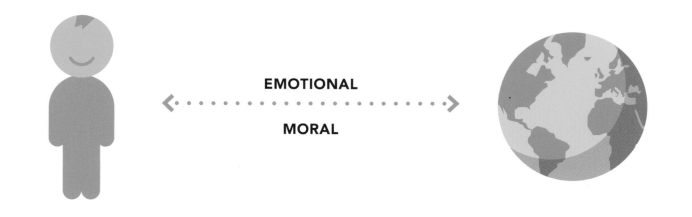

EMOTIONAL

MORAL

EVERY KID IS CHANGING EMOTIONALLY AND MORALLY

At every phase, kids experience emotions and face moral dilemmas. As they grow, kids learn to identify and master their emotions—so eventually they don't scream violently when you won't let them re-chew the gum wad previously stuck under the table. They also develop empathy and compassion in some pretty remarkable ways. The way a kid develops emotionally and morally is connected to how they relationally resolve the conflict points of cultural, mental, and physical changes.

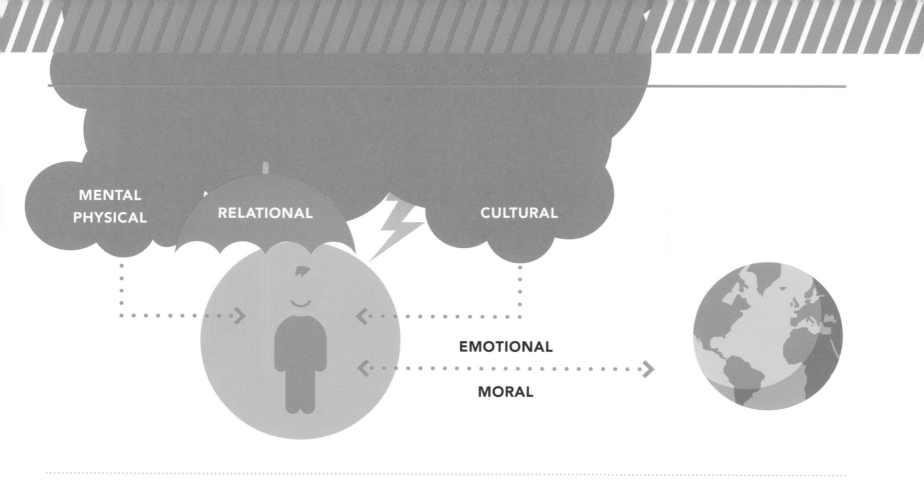

MENTAL
PHYSICAL

RELATIONAL

CULTURAL

EMOTIONAL

MORAL

WE NEED TO UNDERSTAND SIX PRESENT REALITIES ABOUT EVERY KID

Every phase presents new challenges when what is changing mentally and physically collides with what is changing culturally. Relationships help a kid resolve those challenges in a way that shapes their emotional and moral responses.

IF YOU WANT TO
HELP A KID KNOW
THEY MATTER,

GET SERIOUS ABOUT
KNOWING A KID NOW.

6 READ THEIR MIND

SO KIDS AT EVERY PHASE WILL BELIEVE THEY CAN WIN

"Read their mind" is just another way of saying
every leader needs to understand what's changing mentally and physically.

MOST OF THE RESEARCH ON BABIES WILL TRY TO CONVINCE YOU THAT BABIES ARE BRILLIANT.
We naturally underestimate their abilities. They can't feed themselves, soothe themselves, or walk from one place to another. So we have to keep reminding ourselves that babies are also *very* smart.

MOST OF THE RESEARCH ON TEENS WILL TRY TO CONVINCE YOU THEY AREN'T GROWN UP YET.
We naturally overestimate their capacity. They can drive a car, solve an algebra problem, learn a foreign language, and memorize a monologue. So we have to keep reminding ourselves that teenagers aren't really adults—not yet.

The problem is this: If you don't accurately assess the physical and mental characteristics of an age group, you run the danger of expecting them to do more than they're able to do or not really challenging them to do what they can do.

You may have noticed this in your own experience. When activities are too physically demanding or concepts are too difficult to grasp, kids become discouraged and give up. When the activities are too simple and not challenging enough, kids become bored and disinterested. That's why it's important to read their mind.

When you know what can be expected of a phase, you are able to give kids the right amount of success.

In Deuteronomy 6, Moses addressed the nation of Israel and made a passionate plea to "impress" on the hearts of children core truths that relate to God's character. Some translations use the phrase "teach diligently." The phrase can also be translated to mean "to cause to learn." He wasn't advocating a lecture-based, Torah literacy program where a teacher's responsibility ended once they presented the content.

What Moses knew was this. The role of a leader is not to simply present accurate information. The role of a leader is to keep presenting, to keep translating, to keep creating experiences until someone has learned what they need to know.

So your job is simple.

Know what can be expected of them and know how they think
so they will hear what you say and know what to do.

Kids and teenagers don't think like adults. The next pages offer four simple analogies
to summarize the way kids think so you can help them to learn what is most important.

Just remember, when you understand the way a kid's mind is changing,
you stand a far better chance of . . .
identifying clues that help you know what they are thinking.
conveying a message they can understand.
laying a foundation for later learning.

"CHILDREN ARE MOST LIKE ADULTS IN THEIR FEELINGS. THEY ARE LEAST LIKE ADULTS IN THEIR THINKING; MORE INFORMATION DOES NOT MAKE THEM THINK LIKE US."

CATHERINE STONEHOUSE[1]

PRESCHOOLERS

THINK
LIKE AN
ARTIST

ARTISTS EXPERIENCE THE WORLD THROUGH ACTIVITIES THAT STIMULATE THE FIVE SENSES. PRESCHOOLERS BLEND REALITY WITH IMAGINATION AND LEARN THROUGH PARTICIPATION.

A baby's brain has more neurons than at any other time in life, and those neurons are forming two million synapses every second.[2] In this phase, they are mildly aware of everything in their environment, and they take it all in at an unfathomable pace. Preschoolers learn experientially, through their senses, from someone who responds to them. In their world, there is no real distinction between what is real and what is imaginary. Like artists, they learn best when they can make it with their hands. This is why movement, music, and art are critical for learning in this phase.

ELEMENTARY-AGE KIDS

THINK
LIKE A
SCIENTIST

SCIENTISTS UNDERSTAND THE WORLD THROUGH CONCRETE EVIDENCE THEY CAN TEST REPEATEDLY. ELEMENTARY-AGE KIDS DISCOVER HOW THINGS WORK THROUGH REPETITION AND CLEAR APPLICATION.

Brain research suggests that during the elementary years (ages 4-10 or 11), kids learn information quickly and easily.[3] But just because kids in this phase are eager learners doesn't mean they learn like adults. They're still mostly concrete thinkers. They need repetition and clear application. Like a scientist, they learn best when they can observe something in their present environment. The more frequently a new concept can be connected to everyday experience, the better.

MIDDLE SCHOOLERS

THINK
LIKE AN
ENGINEER

ENGINEERS SOLVE PROBLEMS BY CONNECTING CONCEPTS SO THEY WORK TOGETHER. MIDDLE SCHOOLERS PERSONALIZE ABSTRACT CONCEPTS BY CONNECTING IDEAS.

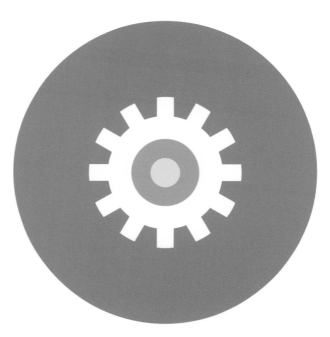

Like their physical bodies, there is a "growth spurt" in the brain of a middle schooler. The brain overproduces neurons and synapses similar to the growing brain of a toddler. This period of rapid growth accounts for a middle schooler's ability to think more abstractly, to understand multiple perspectives, and to think critically about themselves and others. It also means that instructions need to be simple and clear if you hope to be heard. Like an engineer, they learn best when they personalize an idea by connecting pieces of information. That's why puzzles, patterns, and codes can be helpful for learning in this phase.

HIGH SCHOOLERS

THINK
LIKE A
PHILOSOPHER

PHILOSOPHERS SEEK TO UNDERSTAND WHAT IS UNSEEN AND WHAT CANNOT BE MEASURED. HIGH SCHOOLERS WANT TO DISCOVER MEANING AND LEARN BEST BY PROCESSING OUT LOUD.

A high schooler loses approximately one percent of the grey matter of their brain every year through a process called "pruning."[4] Pruning allows the brain to prioritize information to become flexible and efficient. With this new efficiency comes an increase in analytical thinking. But, the limbic system (risk-taking) is developing at a faster rate than the prefrontal cortex (regulating behavior). So risk and personal experience still govern behavior. Like a philosopher, they learn best through open debate, multiple perspectives, and applied reasoning. That's why self-expression and community are essential for learning in this phase.

MENTAL AND PHYSICAL CHANGES

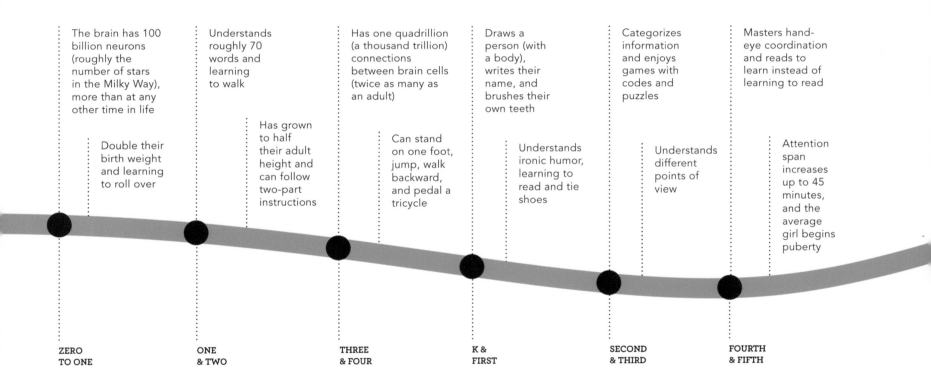

The brain has 100 billion neurons (roughly the number of stars in the Milky Way), more than at any other time in life

Double their birth weight and learning to roll over

Understands roughly 70 words and learning to walk

Has grown to half their adult height and can follow two-part instructions

Has one quadrillion (a thousand trillion) connections between brain cells (twice as many as an adult)

Can stand on one foot, jump, walk backward, and pedal a tricycle

Draws a person (with a body), writes their name, and brushes their own teeth

Understands ironic humor, learning to read and tie shoes

Categorizes information and enjoys games with codes and puzzles

Understands different points of view

Masters hand-eye coordination and reads to learn instead of learning to read

Attention span increases up to 45 minutes, and the average girl begins puberty

ZERO TO ONE

ONE & TWO

THREE & FOUR

K & FIRST

SECOND & THIRD

FOURTH & FIFTH

THINKS LIKE AN ARTIST   THINKS LIKE A SCIENTIST

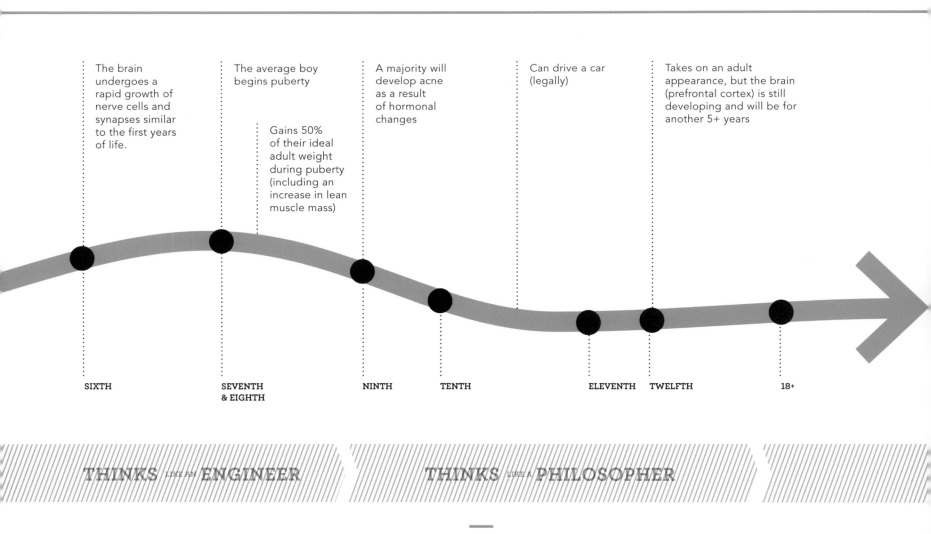

The brain undergoes a rapid growth of nerve cells and synapses similar to the first years of life.

The average boy begins puberty

Gains 50% of their ideal adult weight during puberty (including an increase in lean muscle mass)

A majority will develop acne as a result of hormonal changes

Can drive a car (legally)

Takes on an adult appearance, but the brain (prefrontal cortex) is still developing and will be for another 5+ years

SIXTH

SEVENTH & EIGHTH

NINTH

TENTH

ELEVENTH

TWELFTH

18+

THINKS LIKE AN ENGINEER

THINKS LIKE A PHILOSOPHER

7

DISCOVER THEIR WORLD

SO KIDS AT EVERY PHASE WILL FEEL LIKE THEY BELONG

Every phase has unique cultural changes.
But you can't discover everything you need to know about the culture of childhood and adolescence in a book. By the time a book is printed, culture has changed.

The only way for you to learn some of what you need to know is to . . .
go to their movies,
read their books,
watch their TV shows,
follow their favorite celebrities,
listen to their music,
and most importantly show up where they show up.
From time to time, you might even find yourself at an elementary talent show,
a middle school football game, or a high school play. Think of it as research.

You will never know kids the way you need to know them
if you don't take time to discover their world again and again.

There are other changes in a kid's world that are much more predictable.

For example, a kid's culture changes when they . . .

Are born	Enter elementary school	Enter high school
Become potty-trained	Hit puberty	Get a driver's license
Encounter discipline	Develop abstract thinking	Graduate

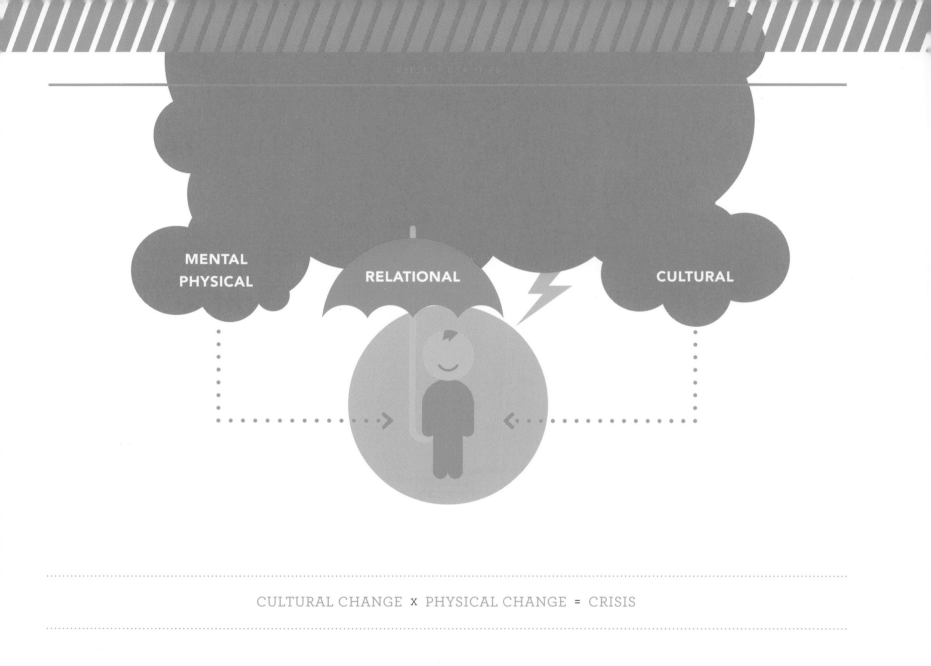

MENTAL
PHYSICAL

RELATIONAL

CULTURAL

CULTURAL CHANGE x PHYSICAL CHANGE = CRISIS

Cultural changes create a platform to discover who we are.

Cultural changes create tension. When they collide with physical and mental changes, it results in a crisis.

Every phase has its own predictable crisis. Unpredictable crises also have influence, but they're less predictable. These crises help shape our identity because they give us an opportunity to navigate new challenges.

Relationships create a safe place to resolve who we are.

Relationships bring clarity. When kids see themselves the way a loving adult sees them, it changes how they see themselves.

DON'T MISS THIS: THE BUFFER IN EVERY CRISIS IS LOVE.

That's why kids and teenagers need adults who will discover their world. They need adults who understand and respond accordingly to the crisis of every phase.

When you misinterpret the crisis of a phase, you risk making a kid feel isolated in a way that may distort the way they see themselves and affect their ability to relate with others.

When you understand the crisis of every phase, you respond with relationships that meet a kid's most basic needs, and you give kids a healthy foundation for future relationships.

The next pages summarize the crisis of each phase by presenting fundamental relational questions every kid needs to answer at every phase.

PRESCHOOL

In the first five years of life, a child forms impressions about themselves and the world. The way a child resolves the "Am I" questions of these phases establishes a critical foundation for their future. It shapes how a child trusts others, how confident they feel about their own abilities, and how they internalize motives for behavior and self-control. **The best way to resolve a preschooler's relational questions is to consistently EMBRACE their physical needs.**

Practically speaking, here's how to do that ·······························➤

AM I SAFE?

In the first year of life, a baby needs to know they are safe. When adults consistently respond to a baby's needs, babies **Establish Trust**.

AM I ABLE?

When a toddler is one and two years old, they discover new abilities. When adults patiently allow toddlers to try new things, toddlers **Develop Confidence.**

AM I OKAY?

When a preschooler is three or four, they learn a few rules and expectations. When adults set boundaries and discipline with love, preschoolers **Cultivate Self-Control.**

ELEMENTARY

In the elementary years, a child develops skills and competencies that equip their future. The way a child resolves the "Do I have" questions of these phases provides them with critical knowledge and resources. It shapes their perception of personal ability, comparative value, and resilience. Through these phases, kids shift from wanting to be seen by adults to wanting to be seen by adults and peers. **The best way to resolve a kid's relational questions is to ENGAGE their interests.**

Practically speaking, here's how to do that

DO I HAVE YOUR ATTENTION?

In Kindergarten and first grade, a child craves adult attention and approval. When adults demonstrate interest in a kid's progress, kids **Improve Abilities.**

DO I HAVE WHAT IT TAKES?

In second and third grade, a kid wants to know how their abilities compare with peers. When adults praise a kid's persistence and efforts, kids **Broaden Competence**.

DO I HAVE FRIENDS?

In fourth and fifth grade, a kid begins to prioritize friends in a new way. When adults make introductions and include peers, kids **Develop Friendships**.

MIDDLE SCHOOL

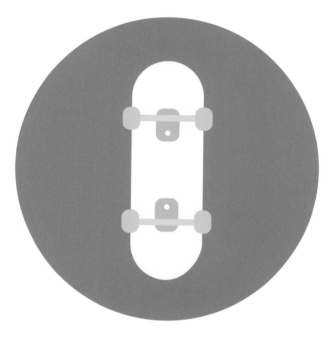

In middle school, a preteen challenges authority and personalizes what they believe. The way a middle schooler resolves the "Who" questions of life determines the framework for their relational stability. It affects the way they see themselves, the way they see the world, and the way they see themselves in the world. In these phases, the relational questions shift from black-and-white to grey. The answers are no longer the same for every kid, so they need to be personalized. **The best way to resolve a middle schooler's relational questions is to AFFIRM their personal journey.**

Practically speaking, here's how to do that • ❯

WHO DO I LIKE?

WHO LIKES ME?

Sixth graders need an overdose of acceptance to combat the storm of changes. When adults recruit other affirming leaders and peers, kids **Gain Stability**.

WHO AM I?

Seventh and eighth graders are increasingly self-aware and self-conscious. When adults acknowledge positive qualities and strengths, kids **Discover Uniqueness**.

HIGH SCHOOL

In high school, a teenager refines their unique abilities and develops a sense of purpose. The way a high schooler resolves the "Where," "Why," "How," and "What" questions of life provides a compass for navigating their future direction. It affects the way they pursue community, live out a personal ethic, and contribute to a greater mission. **The best way to resolve a high schooler's relational questions is to MOBILIZE their potential.**

Practically speaking, here's how to do that • ➤

WHERE DO I BELONG?

Freshmen are looking for a new tribe.
When adults connect teens with similar interests, teens
Value Community.

WHY SHOULD I BELIEVE?
WHY CAN'T I?

Sophomores want to challenge the limits.
When adults listen carefully and respond with questions, teens
Clarify Values.

HOW CAN I MATTER?

Juniors are ready to make a difference—now.
When adults provide consistent opportunities to lead and serve, teens
Refine Skills.

WHAT WILL I DO?

Seniors want to know where they are headed.
When adults encourage experiences and simplify options, teens
Create Vision.

RELATIONAL QUESTIONS

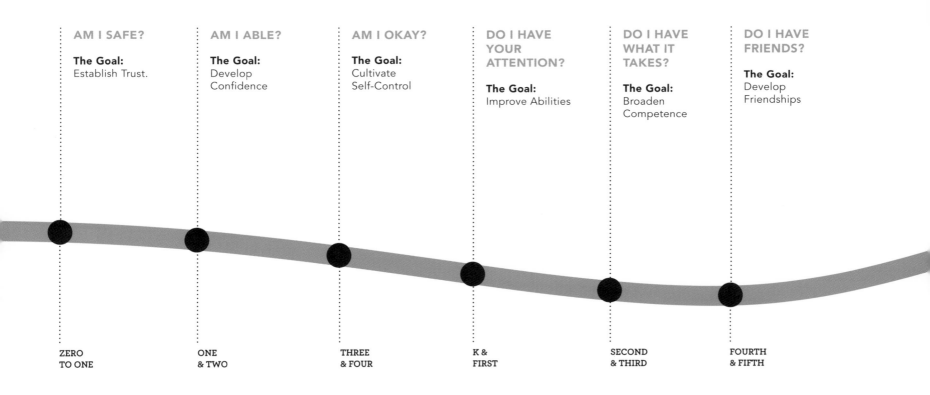

AM I SAFE?

The Goal:
Establish Trust.

AM I ABLE?

The Goal:
Develop
Confidence

AM I OKAY?

The Goal:
Cultivate
Self-Control

**DO I HAVE
YOUR
ATTENTION?**

The Goal:
Improve Abilities

**DO I HAVE
WHAT IT
TAKES?**

The Goal:
Broaden
Competence

**DO I HAVE
FRIENDS?**

The Goal:
Develop
Friendships

ZERO
TO ONE

ONE
& TWO

THREE
& FOUR

K &
FIRST

SECOND
& THIRD

FOURTH
& FIFTH

EMBRACE

ENGAGE

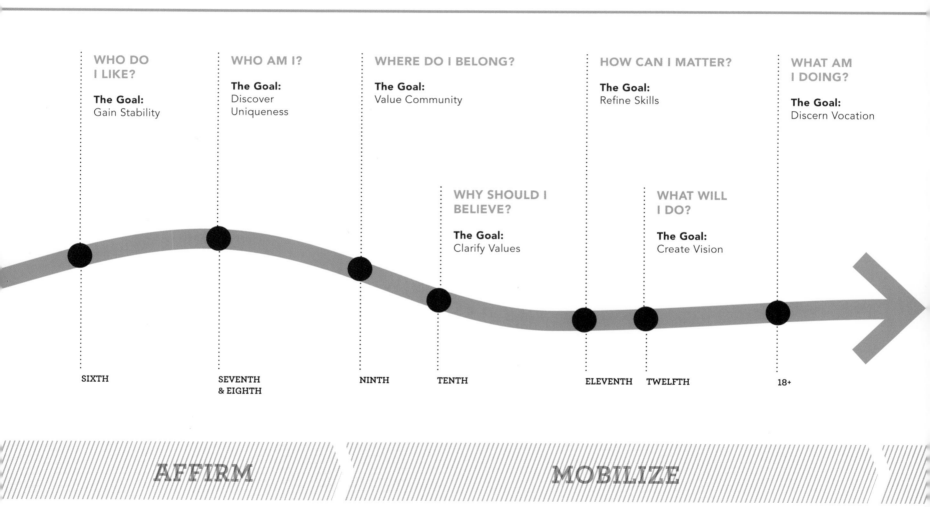

WHO DO I LIKE?

The Goal:
Gain Stability

WHO AM I?

The Goal:
Discover Uniqueness

WHERE DO I BELONG?

The Goal:
Value Community

WHY SHOULD I BELIEVE?

The Goal:
Clarify Values

HOW CAN I MATTER?

The Goal:
Refine Skills

WHAT WILL I DO?

The Goal:
Create Vision

WHAT AM I DOING?

The Goal:
Discern Vocation

SIXTH

SEVENTH & EIGHTH

NINTH

TENTH

ELEVENTH

TWELFTH

18+

AFFIRM

MOBILIZE

INTERPRET THEIR MOTIVES

SO KIDS AT EVERY PHASE WILL DISCERN WHAT THEY SHOULD DO

Growing up has always been hard work.
And it's even more challenging today.

Think for a minute about how . . .
access,
connection,
pressure,
have changed since you were in fifth grade.

Today's generation is growing up in a world where alcohol abuse begins as early as ten years old, the average age to view pornography is eleven, 12-year-olds are prone to self-harm, and suicide is the third-leading cause of death in adolescents. Counselors report a rapidly growing epidemic of depression in teens. Without getting into *why* things are changing, it's important to recognize that they *are* changing.

Kids have to navigate increasingly serious pressures, temptations, and moral dilemmas at an earlier age than ever before.

Maybe that's one reason why—now more than ever—adults who care about the future of the next generation should find ways to help a kid . . .

Make friends
Cooperate with others
Stand up to bullies
Problem-solve

Laugh
Show initiative
Develop integrity
Be resourceful

Show respect
Communicate effectively
Take care of their body
Wait for what they want

Of course, that list could be a lot longer. The science of developing an emotional intelligence and moral foundation is complex. But to oversimplify for a minute, from the time a child is born, they must learn to do four things.

Çô **RECOGNIZE** (Name the emotions they feel)
÷ô **MANAGE** (Take charge of their emotions)
òô **EMPATHIZE** (Recognize the emotions of others)
Ÿô **LOVE** (Respond to others with kindness)

Unlike other developmental milestones, these four skills don't change at every phase. Instead, kids and teenagers are in a continual process of improving the same four things. (Actually, most of us adults are still working through this list, too.)

When it comes to the way kids develop these four skills, there are two things to remember:

1. MENTAL AND PHYSICAL ABILITIES SET THE LIMITS.

Emotional and moral development can't outpace physical development. You can't explain how you feel before you know the words to describe your feelings. You can't make someone dinner before you are old enough to reach the stove. So, remember to consider mental and physical abilities as you set moral and emotional expectations.

2. CULTURAL AND RELATIONAL EXPERIENCES LAY THE FOUNDATION.

When you feel secure with yourself, it's easier to affirm others. When you know where you belong, it's easier to accept others. In the same way, life experience broadens our capacity to relate and empathize. So, you may have to adjust your expectations for moral and emotional development based on each individual child's experience.

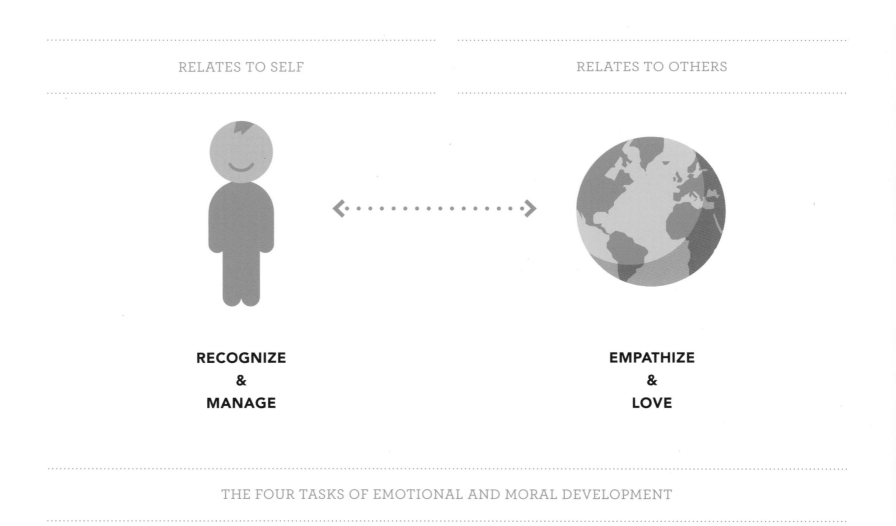

RELATES TO SELF

RELATES TO OTHERS

**RECOGNIZE
&
MANAGE**

**EMPATHIZE
&
LOVE**

THE FOUR TASKS OF EMOTIONAL AND MORAL DEVELOPMENT

Here's something else to consider.

Moral emotions are instinctive.
Moral development is not.

Compassion is part of our genetic code. Babies turn their heads to look at another baby in distress. Toddlers share a favorite toy with a kid who is crying. That's moral emotion. We are born with the capacity to care for others—but so are animals. The natural world is actually filled with similar acts of kindness.

What makes us uniquely human is our God-given ability to manufacture and control our emotions and responses simply by thinking about them. Humans have a distinctive ability to consciously form new thought patterns that transform their brain and affect their behaviors. That's moral development.

This means:
As kids grow, their emotional and moral abilities can either diminish or increase.

Our remarkable ability to understand virtue, to control emotional responses, and to create and uphold moral standards sets the human race apart from the rest of creation. Unlike mental and physical development, moral development doesn't happen automatically. In order for a kid to discover their uniquely created potential—to grow emotionally and morally—they need a guide.

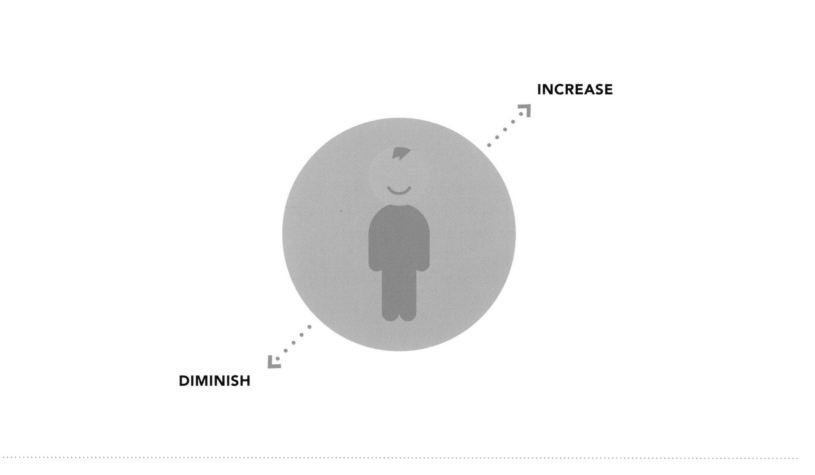

INCREASE

DIMINISH

EMOTIONAL OR MORAL ABILITIES OVER TIME

A guide helps someone become self-aware of the effect their choices and behaviors have on themselves and others.

Kids and teenagers need consistent reinforcement. They need someone who can smile at the good and frown at the bad, so they repeat positive ways of thinking and doing. They need someone who can interpret what is happening in real time, who can assist their decision-making process.

That's why kids and teenagers need the influence of parents and consistent adult leaders. It might also be the reason Scripture says things like . . .
"Train up a child in the way he should go."
"Bring them up in discipline and instruction."
"Train your children because then there is hope."

God designed our emotional and moral formation to require a relational investment. That's also why it's important to help kids grow up and learn how to respond to a relationship with God. He wired every kid so they can know Him as their ultimate guide.

Research and theory around emotional and moral development is complex. There's no one simple formula for how a person grows a moral conscience. But it seems as if helping kids discern what they should do really comes down to one simple factor—understanding their motive.

It's not education. In fact, research has shown again and again that "simple memorization and recitation have little effect on behavior."[5] In other words, simply knowing rules for good behavior isn't enough.

It's not observation. Kids are keen observers, but they are also poor interpreters. There are hundreds of examples of the wrong translations kids make when it comes to their observations about adult moral behavior.

That's not to say leaders shouldn't be good models and teach practical application. They should. It's just that neither one is sufficient for helping kids discern what to do in the complex world they face every day.

If you want to help a kid develop a moral conscience, you have to interpret and influence their motive.

When you influence a kid's current behavior,
you only help them respond to their present circumstance.

But when you influence a kid's motive
you set them up to win in future circumstances.

That's why the role of a guide isn't to motivate a kid or teenager to do right.
The role of a guide is to influence their motives so they can discern what is right.

Motive affects more than temporary behavior. Motive affects the way a person consistently interprets and responds
to the world around them. Maybe that's why motive matters . . .
in a court of law.
in a sibling argument.
in an everyday decision.

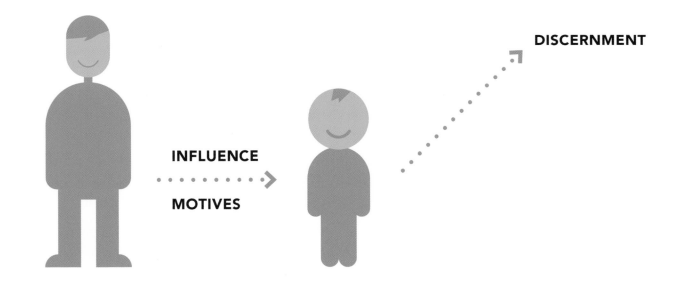

INFLUENCE

MOTIVES

DISCERNMENT

ROLE OF A GUIDE

Interpreting and influencing motives over time helps build character.
We all have a list of virtues, or qualities, that we hope will ultimately drive the way our kids make decisions and treat others. But the truth is every good motive comes back to one.

THE ULTIMATE MOTIVE IS LOVE.

Christians should be leading experts in moral growth. After all, love is the leading fruit of the Spirit, the focus of the Greatest Commandment, and the distinguishing characteristic for being a follower of Jesus.

The point is this. Moral formation begins by influencing motive. And love is the greatest motive. The trouble is . . .

**You can't influence someone's motives
until you know what motivates them.**

And guess what. Most kids don't come preprogrammed with love as their primary motive. In fact, at every phase kids and teenagers have other primary motives at work driving their responses. So, if you want kids to grow emotionally and morally, you need to interpret and respond to their primary motive.

Here's another thing to consider.

**Ultimately, you can't influence someone's motives
unless they know what motivates you.**

Especially as kids get older and become more critical of adult authority, they may question what motivates you. So, if you want their motive to be love, you may have to begin by proving that your motive is love.

Stated another way,
**the best way to help a kid grow up and respond to others from a motive of love
is to guide them in each phase from a motive of love.**

As you influence the motive of kids and teenagers to recognize, manage, empathize and ultimately love, you should begin by loving them enough to know what motivates them. The next pages summarize the primary motive of each phase along with just a few simple developmental thoughts to help guide you as you guide the next generation.

PRESCHOOL

Preschool is a world of action and heightened emotion. Think of it as a training ground for middle school—except they don't have as many words to express their emotions yet. That's why you have to EMBRACE their physical needs. **Preschoolers are primarily motivated by safety.** So if you try to motivate a preschooler with fear, it may work against their primary motive and lead to mistrust and deception. But when you guide them with love, you give a preschooler consistent boundaries in a loving relationship. Then you influence them to trust and respond with obedience to the one who keeps them safe.

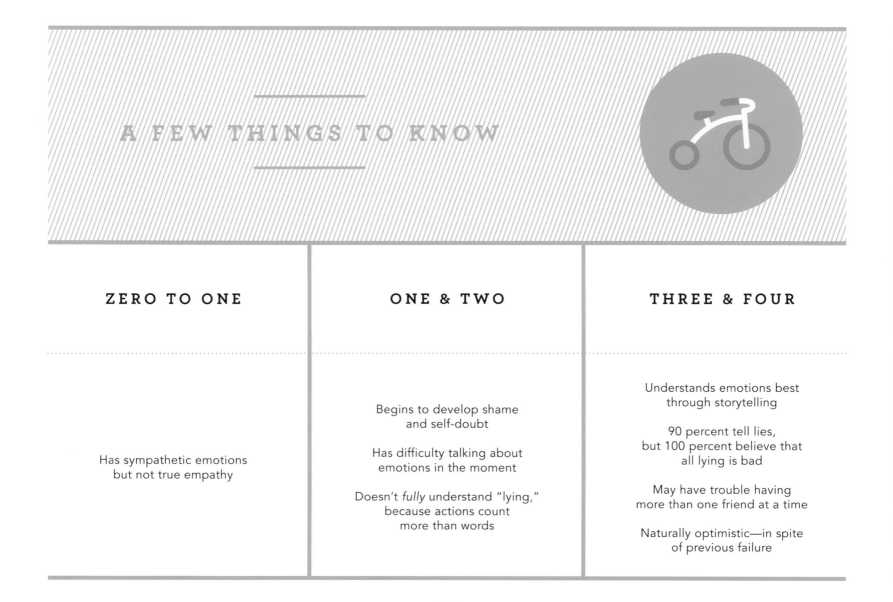

A FEW THINGS TO KNOW

ZERO TO ONE	ONE & TWO	THREE & FOUR
Has sympathetic emotions but not true empathy	Begins to develop shame and self-doubt	Understands emotions best through storytelling
	Has difficulty talking about emotions in the moment	90 percent tell lies, but 100 percent believe that all lying is bad
	Doesn't *fully* understand "lying," because actions count more than words	May have trouble having more than one friend at a time
		Naturally optimistic—in spite of previous failure

ELEMENTARY

Elementary school is a season of discovering how the world works and how to have fun in it. Kids want to laugh and play and learn and connect. That's why you have to ENGAGE their interests. **Elementary-age kids are primarily motivated by fun.** So if you try to motivate kids with too many restrictive rules, it may work against their primary motive and drive them to find enjoyment somewhere else. But when you guide them with love, you introduce transferable principles that will help them win in life and friendship. Then you influence them to make wiser choices and treat others with kindness.

A FEW THINGS TO KNOW

KINDERGARTEN & FIRST

Can name all of the major emotions

Has a hard time regulating fear

Wants to be first and to win

SECOND & THIRD

Often confuses "I feel" with "I am"

Emphasizes fairness and sensitive to blame

"Privacy" becomes a power struggle

FOURTH & FIFTH

Can see the point of view of someone other than themselves

Increased pressure to conform to "norms"

Finds identity in groups like "my team"

MIDDLE SCHOOL

Middle school can be impulsive and intense. Whatever they feel they feel with passion—even if they may change their mind tomorrow. They have a unique blend of confidence and insecurity unlike any other phase. So you have to AFFIRM their personal journey. **Middle schoolers are primarily motivated by acceptance.** If you try to motivate a preteen through shame or embarrassment, it may work against their primary motive and lead to defiant and defensive behavior. But when you respond to them in a loving manner, you learn to listen more often, encourage more specifically, and guide more patiently. Then you influence them to stop and think rationally before they respond in the moment.

A FEW THINGS TO KNOW

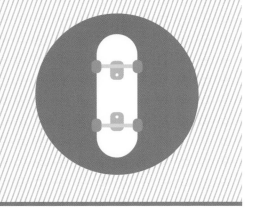

SIXTH

Expands black and white
thinking to consider motive

Expands empathy
beyond just people they know

Understands complex emotions,
but desires to shut them
out in order to fit in

SEVENTH & EIGHTH

The most deceitful age—
they will lie

Begins to integrate
reason and emotion

Able to self-reflect and evaluate

Tends to be preoccupied
with ability (or lack of it)
and undervalue effort

HIGH SCHOOL

High school is a time to test the limits. They are ready for new experiences and desire greater independence from authority. That's why you have to MOBILIZE their potential. **High school students are motivated by freedom.** If you try to motivate a 17-year-old through excessive limits, it may work against their basic motive and incite frustration and rebellion. But when you guide them with love, you collaborate on boundaries and give high school students opportunities to prove they can be trusted. Then you influence them to make responsible decisions and expand their opportunities.

A FEW THINGS TO KNOW

NINTH	TENTH	ELEVENTH	TWELFTH
Feels empowered through choices rather than rules	Responds well to specific praise	Humor is often positive and a sign of leadership skills	Wants to feel ownership of decisions
Wants to create their own solution to a problem	Aware of their personal tendencies and patterns	Lying starts to decline	Still needs support and grace

MORAL DEVELOPMENT

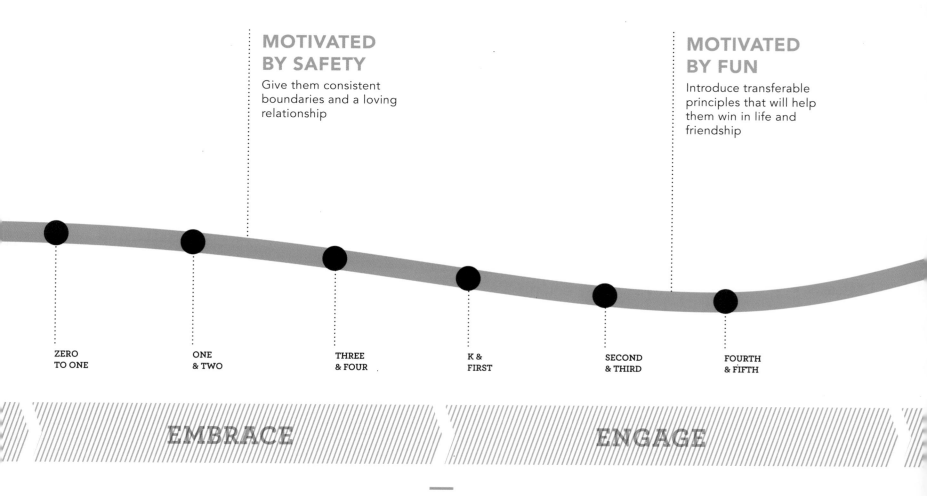

MOTIVATED BY SAFETY

Give them consistent boundaries and a loving relationship

MOTIVATED BY FUN

Introduce transferable principles that will help them win in life and friendship

ZERO TO ONE

ONE & TWO

THREE & FOUR

K & FIRST

SECOND & THIRD

FOURTH & FIFTH

EMBRACE

ENGAGE

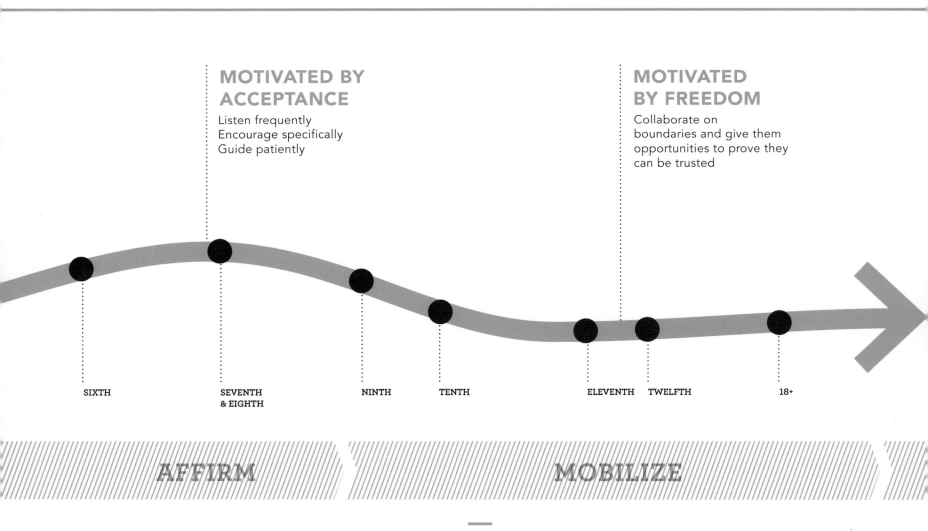

MOTIVATED BY ACCEPTANCE

Listen frequently
Encourage specifically
Guide patiently

MOTIVATED BY FREEDOM

Collaborate on boundaries and give them opportunities to prove they can be trusted

SIXTH   SEVENTH & EIGHTH   NINTH   TENTH   ELEVENTH   TWELFTH   18+

AFFIRM   MOBILIZE

EVERY PHASE HAS

DISTINCTIVE OPPORTUNITIES

YOU NEED TO LEVERAGE

SO

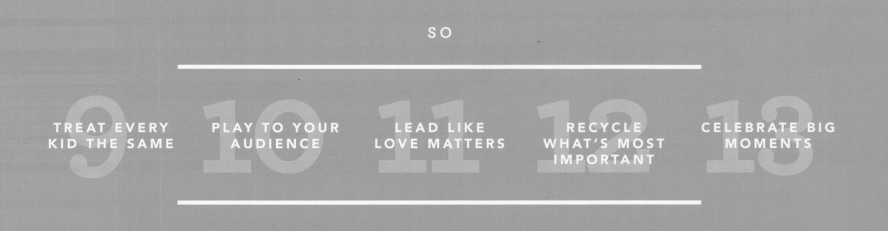

9	10	11	12	13
TREAT EVERY KID THE SAME	PLAY TO YOUR AUDIENCE	LEAD LIKE LOVE MATTERS	RECYCLE WHAT'S MOST IMPORTANT	CELEBRATE BIG MOMENTS

Kids will grow up to have a better future
when three things happen:

They make wise choices.
They build strong relationships.
They have a deeper faith.

Really, the last of those three affects all the rest.

That's why it's up to you to leverage
what's distinctive about every phase.
Because in every phase there are opportunities
to help kids . . .
see their potential to know God.
rediscover how to relate to God.
experience the unconditional love of God.

Then a kid will grow up to understand . . .
God created them,
redeemed them,
and desires to work through them
to love the people around them.

So, don't miss it.
When you show up for kids in every phase
and help them develop authentic faith,
you give them a better future where they
can realize their created potential.

TREAT EVERY KID THE SAME

SO KIDS AT EVERY PHASE WILL SEE THEIR POTENTIAL TO KNOW GOD

A kid has obvious potential the day he or she is born.
Every phase of their life reminds us they
are fearfully and wonderfully made.

Every year the average . . .
toddler will spontaneously burst into over 100,000 giggles.
five-year-old will spout out nearly 160,000 questions.
fourteen-year-old will grow 2 inches and gain 10 pounds.
tenth grader will solve over 1,000 algebra problems.

The point is you should never underestimate a kid's potential to learn, grow, innovate, and believe because there's one thing that makes every kid the same.

Wait.
Isn't the point of this entire book that every kid
at every phase is different?

Sure.
Every phase of a kid's life is very different. And when you add to those differences the fact that each kid has unique DNA, hobbies, quirks, tastes, styles, talents, and opinions, it's safe to say no two kids are alike. Well, sort of.

Think about this:

Every kid doesn't *think* the same, but every kid has the ability to reason.

Every kid doesn't *feel* the same, but every kid wants to be loved.

Every kid doesn't *enjoy* life the same, but every kid loves to have fun.

Every kid doesn't *talk* the same, but every kid has something to say.

Every kid doesn't *look* the same, but every kid likes to be noticed.

Every kid doesn't *imagine* the same, but every kid wants to believe in something.

Why?

At the risk of overstating the obvious to church leaders,

there's one under-emphasized explanation.

EVERY KID IS MADE IN THE IMAGE OF GOD.

Okay. That may not be breaking news to anyone reading this, but stop for a moment

and think about what that really says about every kid around you.

Children have the stamp of God's image imprinted on their lives.

Humans are radically different from every other living, breathing creature.

**EVERY
KID CAN . . .**

LEAD
BELIEVE
IMAGINE
LOVE
CARE
RELATE
TRUST
REASON
IMPROVE

EVERY KID IS MADE IN THE IMAGE OF GOD.

If every kid is created in the image of God
then they have a divine capacity to . . .
believe, imagine, and love.
care, relate, and trust.
reason, improve, and lead.

That's a lot of opportunity to leverage, and you don't want to miss it.

Some adults miss it because they treat kids like they are not . . .
old enough,
smart enough,
mature enough,
important enough,
or even Christian enough
to really learn anything.

But every kid,

| the three-year-old who knows every word of every song in *Frozen*, | the first-grader who knows how to build a Star Destroyer out of Lego blocks, | the third-grader who knows how to spell "interlocutory" at a spelling bee, | the seventh grader who knows how to navigate technology like he invented it, |

has the God-given potential to learn more about God than most adults imagine.

Why? Because every kid is created in the image of God.

What would happen if you just started treating
EVERY KID who breathes like they are created in the **IMAGE of GOD?**

whether they believe what you believe or not
whether they go to church or not
whether they are Christians or not

Just teach every kid . . .
Lead every kid . . .
Influence every kid . . .
like they matter to God
because they are made by God.

Think about it this way:

**When you learn to see God's image in kids,
it increases the potential for kids to see God.**

And when kids begin to understand they are made in the image of God,
they tend to look at the world and themselves in a different way.

This one perspective can affect how they . . .
make decisions.
view sex.
use technology.
relate to their parents.
see the church.
care about people.
trust God.

Don't make the mistake of missing it.
You wouldn't just be ignoring a child.
You could also be ignoring God.
You would definitely be ignoring the potential every kid has to know God.

Maybe that's why Jesus was so emphatic one day
when His disciples were impatient with a group of children.

Jesus knew something the disciples were missing.
That every child is made in God's image.

EVERY
KID CAN . . .

LEAD
BELIEVE
IMAGINE
LOVE
CARE
RELATE
TRUST
REASON
IMPROVE

When they know they are
made in the image of God, it
changes **how they see . . .**

DECISIONS
SEX
TECHNOLOGY
PARENTS
CHURCH
PEOPLE
GOD

EVERY KID IS MADE IN THE IMAGE OF GOD.

Jesus firmly reminded His disciples,
"None of you can really know God or His kingdom,
unless you are willing to trust me like a child."

It's interesting Jesus didn't say kids should become like adults before they can relate to God.
He said adults should learn from kids how to relate to God.

Actually, there may be some ways kids have more potential to know God
and the principles of His kingdom than adults do.

Maybe we program our churches backwards.

WHEN KIDS GROW UP BELIEVING THEY ARE MADE BY GOD,
THEY WILL GROW UP WANTING TO KNOW THE GOD WHO MADE THEM.

Have you ever noticed how kids seem to have an unusual
curiosity and openness to learn about spiritual things?

They don't seem to mind talking *about* God.
They don't seem to mind talking *to* God.

It's interesting.
You typically don't have to prove to a child that God exists.
You just tell them and they believe.
Maybe that's because God Himself wired kids to . . .
imagine,
believe,
and trust from the time they were born.

That's also what makes kids radically different from
elephants and alligators, dogs and cheetahs,
dolphins and eagles, and dragons and unicorns. (You can still imagine too).

Animals don't imagine God.
Animals don't trust what they can't see.
Animals don't pursue spiritual matters.
Animals don't reason about life after death.

But kids do.

They are naturally intrigued with the miraculous supernatural power of a Creator.
They are inquisitive and eager to understand what God is like.
They are openly willing to trust and follow whatever He says.

Moses obviously believed in the potential of kids to believe.

Remember his farewell speech to Israel, when he rallied the entire nation around kids?

What he said became a central thought for all of Jewish and Christian history.

He wanted to make sure kids grew up knowing God,

so he warned leaders and parents to leverage every opportunity

to transfer their faith to their sons and daughters.

One of the most compelling things Moses said was,

"Love the Lord your God with all of your heart, soul, and strength."

In one phrase, he suggested that people who are made in the image of God have the ability

to relate to God through their imagination, intellect, emotions, will, personality, and physical being.

That day, something shifted in the mindset of an entire nation.

God was no longer just an authoritative force to be obeyed.

From that day forward, God was to be viewed as a relational entity

who designed our heart, soul, and even body to help us know and love Him personally.

Since Moses didn't have a childhood development degree, he either had an uncanny ability to understand kids, or he was hearing from God.

You decide.

Moses made his point clear for every parent and leader.

Don't miss the distinct opportunities you have to influence every kid's

"heart, soul, and strength" so they can relate to God.

Think about it this way.

Imagine you have three dials you can turn to help kids connect to God.

Dial #1 is *WONDER*. It affects a kid's thinking and imagination.

This dial represents the Hebrew concept of heart.

Dial #2 is *DISCOVERY*. It affects a kid's emotional and moral development.

This dial represents the Hebrew concept of soul.

Dial #3 is *PASSION*. It affects a kid's skills and relationships.

This dial represents the Hebrew concept of strength.

These dials represent three intrinsic drives that are hardwired in every kid.

Experts in culture obviously know how to appeal to the way kids are designed.

Just watch the latest animated Disney movie, play with the newest educational toy,

listen to the most recent band, or pick up an iPhone.

There has been a lot of research and money spent to understand what drives children.

It's almost as if every kid is wearing an invisible sign that says
Amaze me.
Inspire me.
Move me.

You may think that sounds selfish. Sure, these same drives also have the potential to awaken the dark side of a kid's nature. A kid's attempt to indulge their imagination, satisfy their curiosity, and gratify their physical needs can also lead to things that are damaging and dangerous. Sin could simply be defined as satisfying a God-given drive in an inappropriate way. But just remember God designed these drives to help us.

That's why your role is to . . .
Amaze a kid's mind to imagine God.
Inspire a kid's will to follow God.
Move a kid's life to serve God.

No. That doesn't mean it's up to you to actually make a kid grow spiritually.
That's God's role. You can try. But chances are it will frustrate them and make you tired.
But you should try to get better at breaking up the ground,
planting seeds, watering, and fertilizing a kid's potential to know God.

"LISTEN TO YOUR LIFE. SEE IT FOR THE FATHOMLESS MYSTERY IT IS ... TOUCH, TASTE, SMELL YOUR WAY TO THE HOLY AND HIDDEN HEART OF IT."

FREDERICK BUECHNER

So start treating every kid like they are made in the image of God, with the potential to know and relate to God.
And remember whenever you teach, play, model, discuss, sing, story-tell, pray, worship, or read, you are usually
turning one of three dials.
The better you understand kids at every phase,
the more skilled you can become at knowing how to . . .
Incite Wonder,
Provoke Discovery,
Fuel Passion.

LOVE GOD WITH ALL YOUR . . .

WONDER

DISCOVERY

PASSION

AMAZE ME

INSPIRE ME

MOVE ME

10

PLAY TO YOUR AUDIENCE

SO KIDS AT EVERY PHASE WILL REDISCOVER HOW TO RELATE TO GOD

Imagine going to a U2 concert
with a group of toddlers.

Or buying tickets to see Yo Gabba Gabba
with a middle school group.

Or watching Barry Manilow
with all third grade boys.

Okay, hopefully you have never done any of those things. Musicians, even great musicians, play for a specific audience. Not everyone relates to country music, or hip hop, or jazz. That doesn't make those genres less inspiring. It just means the musician has to know more than music if they hope to connect with their audience.

The same is true if you want to help kids and teenagers connect with their Creator.

Kids at every phase have been made in the image of God with the ability to know God.

But kids at every phase are changing physically, mentally, culturally,
relationally, emotionally, morally—and spiritually

The way a kid relates to God changes at every phase of life.

**Your job is not to redefine God at every phase,
but your job is to help kids rediscover God in a new way at each phase.**

Remember the three drives that are hardwired in every kid?

Wonder   Discovery   Passion

If you think about those drives as dials you turn to help a kid connect with God, then what if you turn those dials to different volumes for different phases?

It's just like finding the right mix for a love song. Wonder is like the melody. Discovery is the harmony. Passion is the rhythm. When you get the mix just right, something magical happens and the song connects with the heart of the listener. That means your role as a leader is to discover the right mix to play for your audience.

The idea of the right mix isn't completely new. Maybe that's why there are *four* different gospels. Matthew was written for a Jewish audience to introduce Jesus as the prophesied Messiah. Luke was written for a Gentile audience to show how Jesus' resurrection was good news for everyone. Mark's a more condensed version. And John focuses on some parts the others don't mention. They tell the same story, but they are mixed with different audiences in mind.

Here's a question. Knowing what you now know about phases . . .
which dial do you think you should turn up the loudest for a preschooler?
which dial do you think you should turn up the loudest for an elementary-age child?
what dial do you think you should turn up the loudest for a middle school or high schooler?

You will turn all three dials at every phase, but the volumes may change in order to create the right mix.

CONSIDER THE WAY EACH AGE GROUP THINKS.

PRESCHOOLERS	ELEMENTARY KIDS	MIDDLE SCHOOLERS	HIGH SCHOOLERS
think like an artist.	think like a scientist.	think like an engineer.	think like a philosopher.

Their world is full of WONDER and imagination.	They combine wonder with DISCOVERY to search for answers.	They blend wonder, DISCOVERY, and passion to solve problems.	They search for meaning and PASSION to discover their place in the world.

Don't misunderstand.
God doesn't change.
But kids do.

Leaders need to think not only in terms of child development, but also spiritual growth. Have you ever stopped to consider what spiritual growth implies? It means something is growing, changing, and moving. It's dynamic.

When it comes to leading the next generation,
spiritual growth means helping kids mature in their ability to relate to God.

In order to grow up and know God at every phase, kids need adults to help them rediscover how to relate to God in every phase. Unfortunately, there are two ways adults unintentionally miss it when it comes to fostering spiritual growth in the next generation.

1. Adults make the mistake of connecting kids and teenagers to a God who seems irrelevant. God is relevant to every phase of life. But there are aspects of God that may feel more relevant at some phases than others. When you leverage distinctive opportunities to influence a kid's faith, you look for ways to appeal to their phase to help them relate to God.

2. Adults make the mistake of connecting kids and teenagers to a God who seems false. That may sound harsh, but with the number of teenagers disconnecting from faith and walking away from church, we need to seriously consider what makes them disconnect. One of those reasons may be that we introduced them to a fixed view of God—the kind of view that believes once you meet God, that's it. You know Him. The problem is as kids grow and change, their perspective and life experience changes. And if they have a view of God that is too fixed, then when something challenges who they thought God was, God may seem like a lie. When you leverage distinctive opportunities to influence a kid's faith, you help them develop a dynamic view of God.

One of the incredible things about a relationship with God is the way He has something unique to show us at every phase. Just like the same dad would respond differently to his three-year-old than his 13-year-old, our heavenly Father seems to respond in different ways at different times so we can better understand how completely He loves us.

That's the funny thing about love. The only way to prove love is to prove it over time, consistently, in spite of what changes. Maybe that's why the story of the world is so similar to the story of our lives.

Think about God's story of love over time.

God **embraced** us as Creator and loving Father.

God **engaged** us as an incarnate Teacher, Leader, and Friend.

God **affirmed** us as a Redeemer and Savior.

God **mobilized** us as a resurrected Christ who gave us His Spirit.

The way God proved His love to humanity through time is similar to the way a child grows up and relates to God throughout the phases.

It's as if there is a pattern for spiritual growth working throughout the events of history the same way it works throughout our lives. Your goal is to show up in the lives of kids and teenagers, over time, to love them and help them mature in their ability to relate to God at every phase.

The best way to help a kid mature in their relationship with God at every phase is to help them relate to God in their present phase.

In every phase you create a unique mix of wonder, discovery, and passion for each phase. Remember that every kid will always need all three—just maybe at different volumes.

HOW PRESCHOOLERS RELATE TO GOD

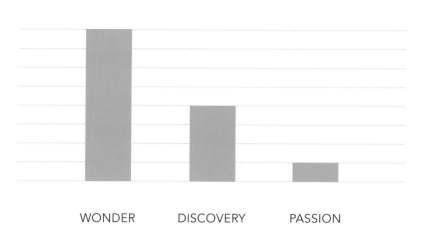

WONDER   DISCOVERY   PASSION

God's Story is My Story

Preschoolers who think like artists blend the stories they hear with the stories they live in a way that makes a loaf and two fish just as memorable as yesterday's pizza. They relate to an invisible God they can imagine. The One who designed the animals and created the flowers, the One who made them and knows everything about them, who keeps them safe, and who loves them.

When you **EMBRACE** their physical needs you help a preschooler know God's love and meet God's family.

THREE IDEAS TO HELP PRESCHOOLERS MATURE IN THEIR RELATIONSHIP WITH GOD

1. **Ignite their imagination.** (*Don't fight it.*) When it comes to the Bible, preschoolers might miss a few details, add some embellishments, or confuse the chronology. Just remember, they aren't overthinking it. They are imagining it. Sometimes it's just better to let them put a monkey in the manger scene and spend your hour talking about the wonder of Jesus being born rather than correcting their historical, geographical understanding of Bethlehem.

2. **Activate their senses**. Artists learn through their senses, so if you really want to help them relate: Sing songs (the more rhyming the better), tell stories with hand motions, make crafts, show videos, use pictures, eat snacks. (Don't worry about creating new smells; there are already enough of those.)

3. **Structure their experience.** Artists may have a reputation for being free spirits, but creativity sometimes flourishes with a little structure. In the same way, preschoolers will feel safe enough to imagine and wonder about their Creator when they know what to expect. So prepare ahead of time. Recruit consistent leaders. Keep the environment clean. Have a set schedule for your experience. Oh, and one more thing. As you set that schedule, remember the attention span of the average three-year-old is about eight minutes. So, plan your time accordingly.

HOW ELEMENTARY-AGE KIDS RELATE TO GOD

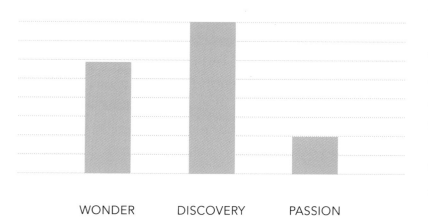

WONDER   DISCOVERY   PASSION

God's Story Inspires My Story

Kids who think like scientists love stories—especially those that inspire them to win at every day life. They relate to a God who heals the sick, conquers evil, explains mysteries, performs miracles, overcomes death, and teaches them how to win at life.

When you **ENGAGE** their interests you help a kid trust God's character and experience God's family.

THREE IDEAS TO HELP ELEMENTARY-AGE KIDS MATURE IN THEIR RELATIONSHIP WITH GOD

1. **Tell one story.** *This* is the age for story. Kids know the difference between history and fiction—and they obsess about what is true. They still have enough wonder to be carried away with the plot, but they are ready to discover what the story means practically and personally. Just like a scientist studies one idea at a time, kids master individual concepts at this phase. Give kids one story and connect it with one concrete idea.

2. **Use real illustrations.** Scientists like concrete evidence. They rely on what they can observe. In the same way, a kid understands what is familiar to their world. Avoid abstract metaphors. When you ask a concrete-thinking child, "Do you want Jesus to come live in your heart?", expect questions like "Where does He sleep in there?" Use visual illustrations to help kids relate to God, and look for ways to connect your illustrations to what they experience every day.

3. **Make it fun.** No one knows how to party like a scientist. Okay, maybe this is where the analogy breaks down. But kids *do* love to have fun. Fun may look different for different kids. Engage their interests by adding variety to your program. Play games with movement. Use maps and puzzles. Give them opportunities to read and write. Go outside when you can—or bring the outside into your space. Sing and dance together. You only have a limited amount of time together, so make it fun enough to remember.

HOW MIDDLE SCHOOLERS RELATE TO GOD

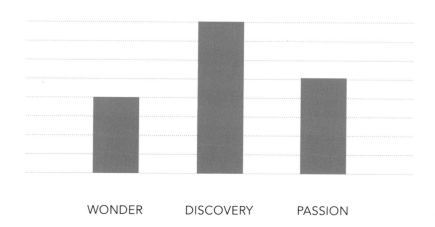

WONDER   DISCOVERY   PASSION

God's Story Redeems My Story

Tweens who think like engineers need to know that God can rebuild a story—even when things haven't gone according to the plan. They relate to a God who overcomes impossible odds to rebuild what is broken, bring stability, restore peace, resolve doubt, give hope, and redeem everyone.

When you **AFFIRM** their personal journey you help a middle schooler own their own faith and value a faith community.

THREE IDEAS TO HELP MIDDLE SCHOOLERS MATURE IN THEIR RELATIONSHIP WITH GOD

1. **Connect the dots.** An engineer may have to connect physics and design in order to solve a problem. In the same way, this is the phase when a kid begins connecting the information they learned in childhood to see how it works together. That means this is the very best phase to connect the overarching narrative of Scripture. There is incredible potential to re-engage their sense of wonder about the Bible when their eyes are open to the masterful way the story connects not only from Genesis to Revelation, but with their own life as well.

2. **Expect a crisis.** When engineers try to solve complex problems in creative ways, a few crisis moments are inevitable. Some middle school crises may seem less complex—like when they're selected to go onstage for "Duct Tape Round-Up." They may also begin to discover they believe a lot of things that don't easily fit together. They may ask how an all-powerful God allows bad things to happen. You won't know all the answers, so don't act like you do. Just affirm what you do know. Help them anchor their faith to what is constant.

3. **Be consistent.** Speaking of constant, you may never have a phase where predictability matters more. Practice making regular promises and following through in simple ways to prove you can be trusted. It may seem like they are testing you. They are. Absolutely nothing you say will matter for a middle schooler unless you say it with the credibility you earn simply by showing up in their world to prove you care.

HOW HIGH SCHOOLERS RELATE TO GOD

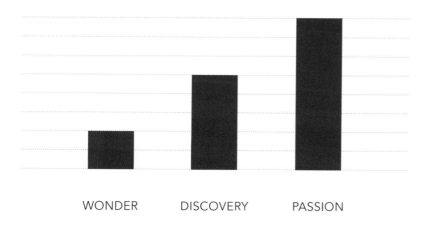

WONDER   DISCOVERY   PASSION

God's Story Empowers My Story

Teenagers who think like philosophers look for principles that will give their story meaning. They relate to a God who guides their decisions, promotes love and forgiveness, empowers their freedom, enables them to live more fully, moves them toward a greater purpose and identity, and connects them to a bigger story.

When you **MOBILIZE** their potential you help a high schooler keep pursuing authentic faith and discover a personal mission.

THREE IDEAS TO HELP HIGH SCHOOLERS MATURE IN THEIR RELATIONSHIP WITH GOD

1. **Give an application.** Don't let the term philosopher confuse you. High schoolers want more than theory. They want to know what is helpful for life right now. The best way to help a high schooler remember what you say is to say something they can do this week. Then maybe post what you said to their social media channel mid-week just as a reminder.

2. **Ask a question.** Philosophers ask questions. If they aren't asking you hard questions, they are asking someone else. That's what high schoolers do. They want to know how what you say connects with their real-world experience. Resist the temptation to defend or overexplain your theology. Anything you talk them into now, someone else can talk them out of later. Give them space. Answer their questions with another question. Guide them to discover the answer on their own if you want it to stick.

3. **Make it experiential.** High schoolers will never feel important until you give them something important to do. They are ready for freedom. They want to do something that matters. They want a little less conversation and more action in their life. Now is the time to give students every opportunity to use their skills to serve and be the Church while they are still with you.

THE RIGHT MIX

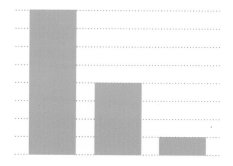

wonder discovery passion

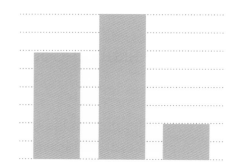

wonder discovery passion

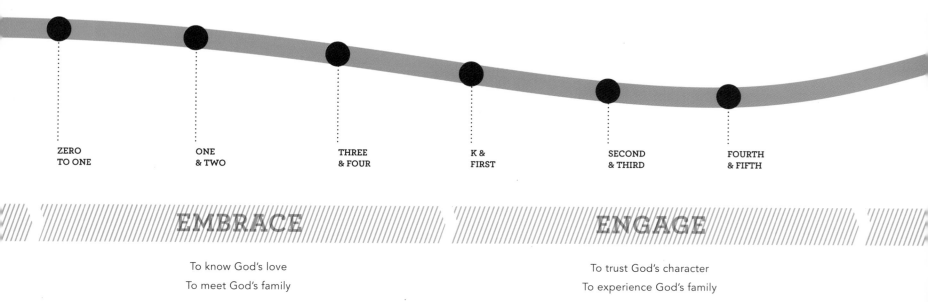

| ZERO TO ONE | ONE & TWO | THREE & FOUR | K & FIRST | SECOND & THIRD | FOURTH & FIFTH |

EMBRACE

To know God's love

To meet God's family

ENGAGE

To trust God's character

To experience God's family

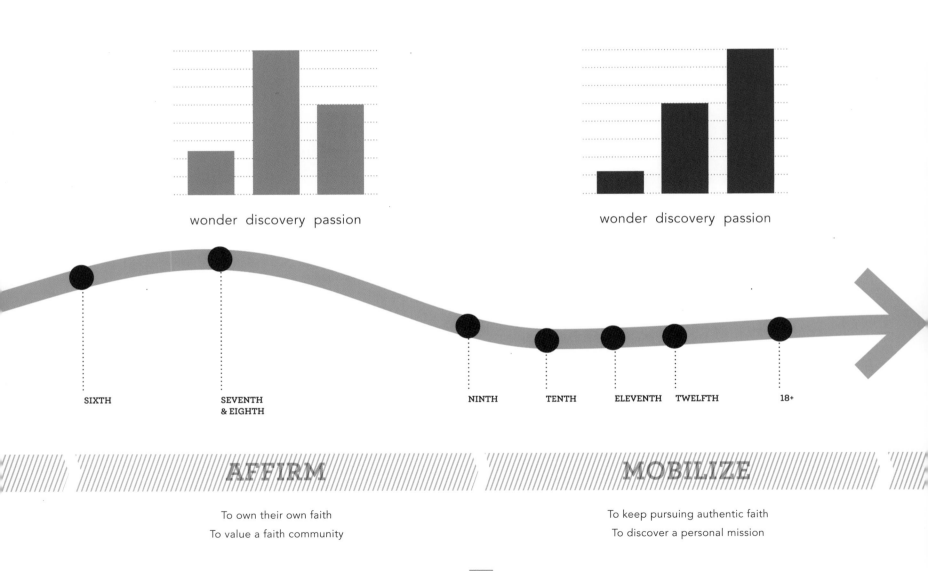

wonder discovery passion

wonder discovery passion

SIXTH

SEVENTH
& EIGHTH

NINTH

TENTH

ELEVENTH TWELFTH

18+

AFFIRM

MOBILIZE

To own their own faith

To value a faith community

To keep pursuing authentic faith

To discover a personal mission

11

LEAD LIKE
LOVE MATTERS

SO KIDS AT EVERY PHASE CAN
EXPERIENCE GOD'S LOVE

Has it ever occurred to you that basically every parent and leader wants the same thing for their kids?
A better future

Regardless of their religion, background, ethnicity, or nationality every parent hopes their son or daughter will have the best future. If you asked leaders and parents to prioritize, it could range anywhere from good friends, to a college education, to a decent job, to a happy marriage, to a Christian faith, and even an Apple computer.

But if you organize everything that is on their list, you could get the specifics down to three major categories:
Smarter decisions
Stronger relationships
Deeper faith

And not necessarily in that order.

By the way, have you ever noticed how a lot of important things happen in threes?
Hope, Faith, and Love
Purpose, Belonging, and Identity
Earth, Wind, and Fire
Scattered, Smothered, and Covered
Father, Son, and Holy Spirit
Wonder, Discovery, Passion

Nearly two thousand years ago, some religious leaders asked Jesus about what mattered most in life. Not because they really wanted to know, but so they could make a point.

These religious leaders had a pretty staunch reputation.
No one worked harder at keeping the rules than they did.
No one showed up at the temple more consistently than they did.
No one prayed longer and harder than they did.
No one studied the Scriptures more than they did.

The Pharisees were always looking for opportunities to flex their theological muscles. So they asked their question in front of a crowd to hopefully gain some fans and to make Jesus look bad,
"You are a teacher with integrity, what do you think is the greatest commandment?"

It's interesting that when Jesus responded, He actually quoted Moses,
"The greatest commandment is to love the Lord your God with all of your heart, mind, soul, and strength."

That answer should not have been a surprise to the Pharisees. They were experts in the law. This commandment was not new. It was thousands of years old. It was considered the *shema* of the Jewish people. This is what Moses had said in his last message to the Hebrew nation. This was the passage Jews had put on the doorposts of their homes for generations and taught their children to memorize. It was like Jesus was giving them their moment in the sun. They were Pharisees. If there was anyone who loved God with all of their mind and with their strength and with their heart, it was a Pharisee.

Here's the context. There was a wide range of people who had come to hear Jesus that day who were listening to the conversation: tax collectors, prostitutes, and all your other average sinners.

If you had been standing in the crowd when the Pharisees asked Jesus the question, "What's the Greatest Commandment?," and you heard Jesus respond, "Love God with everything in your life," you would have thought, "Okay. Pharisees win. I lose." For a brief second, Jesus earned the religious experts a few extra points in front of the rest of the crowd.

It was as if the Pharisees had tricked Jesus into saying, "Just love God with everything in your life. Do what Moses said. Be like a good Pharisee!"

But then it happened. As fast as Jesus had seemed to support their cause, He said something that caught everyone off guard. He added something to the *shema* that had never been added before. (Of course Jesus was qualified to do that since He was God.)

Jesus reached into the six hundred plus laws of the ancient writings of Moses, pulled out an isolated verse, and attached it to what they thought they knew. He basically said, "Oh, one more thing. There's a second part to the Greatest Commandment that's just as important as the first part."

"LOVE YOUR NEIGHBOR AS YOURSELF."

The first part of His answer was like throwing a fastball down the middle to give someone a false sense of timing. Then He threw a curve they never saw coming. It was like Jesus was saying, "You need to learn how to love God. But don't fool yourself into thinking you love God just because you are behaving religiously. The real evidence of whether or not you love God is not by how much you know the Scriptures or how often you go to the temple. The authentic test of your faith is how you treat people. Maybe even some of the actual people standing here."

The Pharisees were good at pretending to love God, but they didn't have a great reputation for loving people. **You can't really love God if you don't love who God loves . . . at least according to Jesus.**

Jesus took what Moses had said about how you relate to God and expanded it to include how you relate to others. He appealed to the image of God in everyone to love God in such a way that it would affect how they loved others. Then He went even a little further to solidify how important this idea really is. He explained to the Old Testament scholars,

"All the law and prophets hang on this commandment."

In other words, Jesus summarized everything with one concept. He reorganized the writings of Moses and the prophets, the major commandments, and every sacred word of the text of the Holy Scriptures into one overarching idea.

LOVE

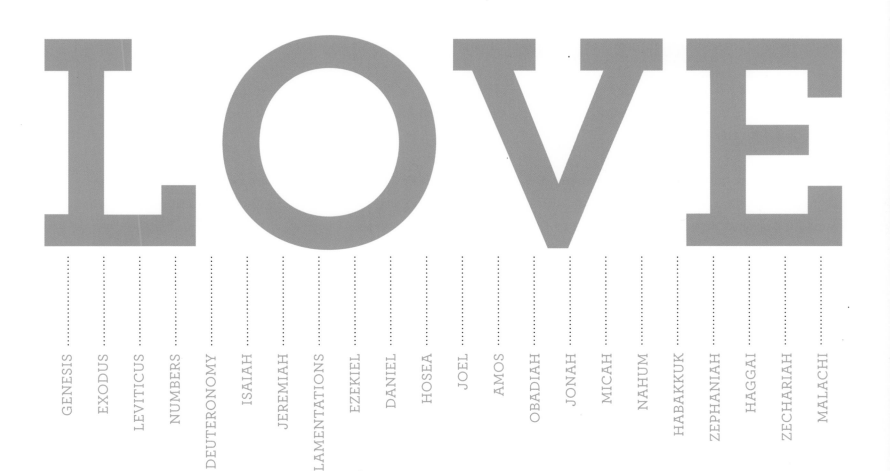

LOVE

GENESIS · EXODUS · LEVITICUS · NUMBERS · DEUTERONOMY · ISAIAH · JEREMIAH · LAMENTATIONS · EZEKIEL · DANIEL · HOSEA · JOEL · AMOS · OBADIAH · JONAH · MICAH · NAHUM · HABAKKUK · ZEPHANIAH · HAGGAI · ZECHARIAH · MALACHI

Jesus made it clear that faith is not about rules, but about responding to a relationship.

Jesus suggested that faith in God has less to do with believing a list of theological truths, and more to do with knowing and loving God. Everything in life comes back to how you relate to God, how you relate to yourself, and how you relate to others.

Later this one thought would be the focus of what James and Paul would both reemphasize as the Royal Law. It would become as central to Christian faith as the *shema* was to Hebrew faith. It would be the primary way to measure our response to the grace and forgiveness of God in our lives.

Let's paraphrase . . .

LOVE MATTERS.

Let's amplify it . . .

LOVING GOD MATTERS.
LOVING YOURSELF MATTERS.
LOVING PEOPLE MATTERS.

And all are true at the same time.

The Great Commandment is a genius way of summarizing God's agenda. Of course it is. It came from the One who made you in His image. And before you get too opinionated about an overemphasis on LOVE, remember who said it. Be careful you don't minimize what Jesus maximized.

Jesus brought everything right back to what Moses said with a brand new twist.

Just keep turning the Wonder, Discovery, and Passion dials. Your role is to help kids
1. Relate to God in such a way that affects how they
2. Relate to others, and
3. Relate to themselves.

Isn't this the future you want for every kid?

WHEN KIDS LOVE GOD ·····················> IT LEADS TO A DEEPER FAITH.

WHEN KIDS LOVE GOD ·····················> IT LEADS TO LOVING OTHERS.
WHEN KIDS LOVE OTHERS ·····················> IT LEADS TO STRONGER RELATIONSHIPS.

WHEN KIDS LOVE GOD ·····················> IT LEADS TO LOVING THEMSELVES.
WHEN KIDS LOVE THEMSELVES ·····················> IT LEADS TO SMARTER DECISIONS.

When you lead kids to follow Jesus, you tend to define faith in terms of a relationship.
Here's a definition of faith you might consider in the light of the Great Commandment:
"Trusting Jesus in a way that transforms how you love God, yourself, and others."

That's why you should take your cue from Jesus if you want to set your kids up for a better future.
That's why it's important to appeal to the image of God in every kid.
That's why it's important to help every kid understand what it means to trust and follow Jesus.
(That's also why it's important to treat kids like you actually believe they are made in the image of God before you try to lead them to follow Jesus.)

Your job is to simply cooperate with the mission of Jesus to demonstrate
God's story of love and forgiveness to the human race.

Okay. Let's recap that story again.
God created Adam, the original man in His image.
Then Adam sinned and made a mess of God's image.
So God decided to become a human and show everyone how much He loved the people
who were made in His image.

That's why Paul refers to Jesus as the second Adam.
Jesus came to fix what the first Adam messed up.
And that's exactly what Jesus did.

JESUS

TRANSFORMS

LOVE

SELF ←········· GOD ·········→ OTHERS

Jesus lived a life that MODELED the image of God.

He forgave prostitutes.

He touched lepers.

He fed the hungry.

He talked to children.

He partied with outcasts.

He treated everyone like they mattered to God.

He recognized the image of God in them because He was God.

Jesus taught in a way that APPEALED to the image of God in every person.

He said things like…	Then He told stories about…
"Blessed are the peacemakers."	a lost son.
"Let your light shine."	a generous widow.
"Do good works."	a loving father.
"Love your enemies."	a good shepherd.

He challenged everyone to treat people like they mattered to God.

Jesus died so that He could REDEEM the image of God.

He allowed himself to be . . .

accused,

judged,

humiliated,

whipped,

and executed,

even though He was innocent and everyone else was guilty.

He demonstrated with His death that the image of God in every person is worth redeeming.

Jesus rose again and is TRANSFORMING us into the image of God.

He proved when He came back to life that He was God.

So now the same God who . . .

made us in His image,

died for us,

and is living again

wants everyone to trust and follow Him.

Why? So He can start re-creating and transforming us back into the image of God to love Him the way He originally designed us to love Him.

That's the story we are telling kids every time we lead them.

The story of what God did *for* me to *redeem* me.
The story of what God is doing *in* me to *transform* me.
The story of what God is doing *through* me to *influence* others.

That's God's story, my story, and our story.
That's wonder, discovery, and passion.
That's loving God, loving myself, and loving others.

That's what we want to do every week in every phase of every kid's life.

So when they walk away one day, their faith will not be defined by what they do, but instead it will be determined by who they love.

"LOVE IS ALWAYS LOUDER.
NO MATTER WHAT.
EVEN IF HATE HAS A BULLHORN.
LOVE IS LOUDER."

KID PRESIDENT

12

RECYCLE WHAT'S MOST IMPORTANT

SO EVERY KID AT EVERY PHASE WILL REMEMBER WHAT YOU WANT THEM TO KNOW

Okay. Let's do some math.
More than likely, the average sixth graders who are coming to your church
will actually come less than 50 percent of the time.

That means they will spend about 25 hours in your church this year.
Of those 25 hours, at least 30 percent will be spent . . .
getting into the room,
saying "hi" to friends,
playing games,
updating their social media,
and saying "bye" to friends.

So that means they will actually experience less than 20 hours
of teaching or small group interaction in a given year.

The reality is that your middle schoolers
will use their smartphone more in one week
than they will attend your church in one year.

So here's the question:
If you have less than 20 times
to connect to a sixth grader this year,
what are you going to teach them?

Are you going to take them chronologically through the entire Bible?
Are you going to cover your denomination's 14 core doctrines?
Are you going to teach verse-by-verse through the book of Habakkuk?
Are you going to amplify whatever your lead pastor is speaking about on Sunday?

Even if you are in denial and still convinced most of your sixth graders
will show up 52 times this year, you still won't find the best option in the list above.

Whenever you add up the actual amount of time you have to influence the spiritual direction of
a kid's life, it could make your task seem daunting and even impossible.

Think about it this way.
This year, the average middle schooler will spend over . . .
200 hours studying math in school.
300 hours watching TV or movies.
600 hours using a mobile phone.

But in the most ideal of scenarios, you will only get about 40 hours in a year to tell that same middle schooler
everything they need to know about God, Jesus, faith, forgiveness, grace, love, life, and eternity.

So what's the plan?
How are you going to influence the spiritual direction of the average child or teenager
when you only have a few minutes every other week?

You could increase your time with each kid if you . . .
build a Christian school,
show up for dinner at their house once a week,
start a 6 a.m. Bible study before school,
bring back lock-ins,
crusade against competitive sports on Sunday,
force every parent to sign a 52-week contract,
or add mid-week programming.

Or
you could rethink your strategy to make the most of the limited time you will have at every phase.

Think about it. Churches usually organize their content for kids in a few different ways.
- They arrange stories of the Bible chronologically.
- They arrange stories so they can emphasize the gospel every week.
- They arrange stories so they can reinforce what following Jesus looks like in everyday life.
Some churches do a combination of all three.

None are right or wrong.
The critical question is how can you be more strategic and relational?

Regardless of which scenario you use, there are still three critical questions
you should address if you want kids to remember what you teach.
1. What is the one thing you want a kid to grow up and never forget?
2. What other core insights do you want them to understand related to that one thing?
3. What is the plan to recycle those insights so kids will remember them?

All of these questions mean you have to make a difficult choice when it comes to your message.

You have to choose what to say and what not to say at every phase.
You have to develop the skill of prioritizing truth.

When you recycle what is most important, it simply means you decide what stories and principles are the most important to highlight at each phase, and then design a content calendar that effectively recycles that content.

Carefully consider the following statement:
**It's not really your job to teach everything that's
in the Bible to every kid at every phase.
It's your job to teach the most important things
in the phase when they matter most.**

Before you slam this book shut because we didn't just say
you should teach the Bible cover-to-cover, just think about it for a minute.
When you take into account the time limits we mentioned above,
it's not possible or practical to teach the entire Bible to any kid.

1189

CHAPTERS

IN THE

BIBLE

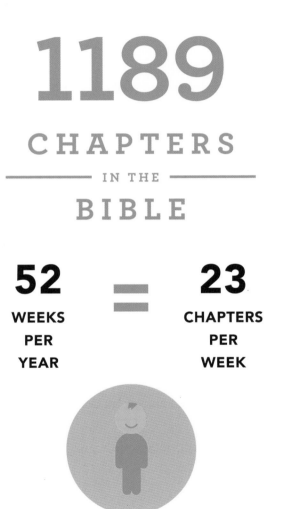

52

WEEKS
PER
YEAR

=

23

CHAPTERS
PER
WEEK

THAT'S A LOT OF CHAPTERS!

**Just because everything in the Bible is equally true
doesn't mean everything in the Bible is equally important.**

That brings us back to what Jesus said to the Pharisees
when they asked Him which commandment was the greatest.

What Jesus *did not say* made a very obvious point.

He didn't answer their question with, "All the commandments of God are equally important, so there is not one commandment that is the greatest." Instead He prioritized what was most important by explaining the Great Commandment. Then He re-organized the rest of the Bible around that idea. As we illustrated in the last chapter, He clearly stated, "All the law and prophets hang on this commandment."

Every once in a while, an idea comes along that is so big, it becomes a **primary organizing factor**. In one statement, Jesus settled thousands of years of theological debate about what really matters when it comes to life and faith. He told us that everything should come back to this concept of loving God.

So what if you simply decided to organize what you teach the way Jesus said it's already organized anyway?

What if you hang all of your content
this week, this year, this decade
on what Jesus said matters most?

It's simple.
Just make sure every story, every principle, and every truth reinforces
for everyone what it means to love God and love others.

Jesus says your content should be organized around a **relational motive**. Love.
When you really think about it, every commandment, every principle, every parable, every story,
and every doctrine can be easily arranged to reflect how you love God, others, and yourself.

Love is the ONE thing that matters most.

Love is the distinctive motive of God's story throughout the Bible.
It's why God made us in His image,
so He could love us and we could love Him.

Love is the distinctive message of the gospel of Jesus.
Jesus lived to model God's love.
Jesus died to prove God's love.
Jesus rose again to empower us with God's love.

Love is the distinctive mark of the church.
Just ask Paul or James. They both agreed.
That's why they reposted what Jesus said in their letters to the church.
They referred to Jesus' commandment to love as the "Royal Law,"
as if to say this idea belongs at the top of everything.

Back to the issue of your limited time.

If you only have a toddler, or a sixth grader, or a teenager for a few times a year,

what is the one thing you don't want them to miss?

Think about it another way.

Every leader and parent hopes their kids will grow up . . .

loving God,

loving others,

and loving themselves

in a healthy way.

What if you simply made sure the one thing you want every kid and teenager

to walk away and know is the one thing that Jesus said was most important?

And what if you decided that what Jesus said is so important, you positioned

everything else you say to reinforce that one thing?

It makes sense really.

You don't want to miss the opportunity

to make sure they don't miss something really big.

You don't want them to miss that the foundation of their faith is a relationship—not information.

That's why any content we give them should be organized to reinforce their relationship with God.

LOVE

SELF ← · · · · · GOD · · · · · → OTHERS

With that in mind, how would you organize core Scriptural insights in a way that could help kids understand how to love God?

WONDER

If you draw three columns to represent the three dials we have already discussed, the first column would obviously represent God. So what are some of the most important things you can make sure a kid understands about God's character? The list below shows one main idea and three supporting thoughts every kid should embrace. You can add to this list if you want. Keep these ideas in mind as you turn the **WONDER** dial in their life so you can help kids understand **"Who is God?"**

I AM CREATED TO PURSUE AN AUTHENTIC RELATIONSHIP WITH MY CREATOR.

Wonder Insight #1

What I see around me reveals a Creator I cannot see.

This means the created world gives every kid evidence to prove that God exists,
is all-powerful, and all-knowing.

Wonder Insight #2

I am created in the image of my perfectly heavenly Father who has an unending love for me.

This suggests that every kid was made by God to experience His love for them.

Wonder Insight #3

I live in pursuit of an infinite God who desires an eternal relationship with me.

This implies that every kid needs to recognize that God is at work in their life to help them know how to love Him.

DISCOVERY

The second column illustrates how God helps a kid discover what it means to follow Jesus and grow in how they see themselves. Keep these ideas in mind as you turn the **DISCOVERY** dial in their life so you can help kids discover *"Who Am I?"*

I BELONG TO JESUS CHRIST AND DEFINE WHO I AM BY WHAT HE SAYS.

Discovery Insight #1
I believe in Jesus and will continually trust Him even when life doesn't make sense.
This means every kid has an opportunity to trust in what Jesus did when He died for their sin and rose again to redeem them. They can be forgiven by Him, and He promises to never stop loving them.

Discovery Insight #2
God's Spirit is transforming my unique and imperfect life into the character of Jesus.
This suggests that God's Spirit is at work changing the heart, soul, and life of every kid who believes in Jesus so they have the power to do what is good and right, and to become more like Jesus.

Discovery Insight #3
My response to God's Word shapes how I see God's story of redemption at work in me and around me.
This implies that God has a bigger story He wants every kid to understand and live out by applying the truths He has explained in His Word.

PASSION

The third column identifies ways God helps kids love others and experience what it means to participate in His mission. Keep these ideas in mind as you turn the **PASSION** dial in their life so you can help kids resolve **"Why Am I Here?"**

I EXIST EVERY DAY TO DEMONSTRATE GOD'S LOVE TO A BROKEN WORLD.

Passion Insight #1
God designed me to participate with Him in restoring a broken world.
This means every kid's calling and mission should be connected to the mission of Jesus to redeem the world.

Passion Insight #2
My faith in Christ is revealed by my compassion and care for others.
This suggests faith is most genuine and authentic in every kid when they are showing compassion and caring for others the way Jesus did.

Passion Insight #3
I choose to live in the complexities of family and community because God values them.
This implies that every kid should recognize God designed the family and church as the primary influences to shape their faith.

Whether you customize this list or make your own, you should decide on the core insights that you want a kid to understand. Then organize those insights in a way that influences a kid's relationship with God, themself, and others. This keeps every kid focused on the value of their relationship with God.

Then you can start answering the next question.
What is the plan to recycle those insights so kids will remember them?
Once you know the core insights you want a kid to grow up and remember, you need a plan for how you will communicate those insights. That's really what "recycling what's most important" means. And if you are going to recycle what's most important, you need to think about content as a "scope and cycle."

Scope: A comprehensive plan that *prioritizes* **what you teach**
Cycle: Your plan to *recycle* **and** *reinforce* **what you teach so it's effective**

When you think in terms of cyclical learning, you recognize core truths will take on fresh meaning with every new phase. Your scope prioritizes what you will teach and your cycle strategically reinforces those principles again and again, in a variety of creative ways.

A "scope and cycle" helps you maximize the limited time you have with the average kid.
It's important for everyone to . . .
stay focused on the one thing that is most important,
identify the core insights that reinforce what is most important,
and follow a plan for when and how those insights will be recycled.

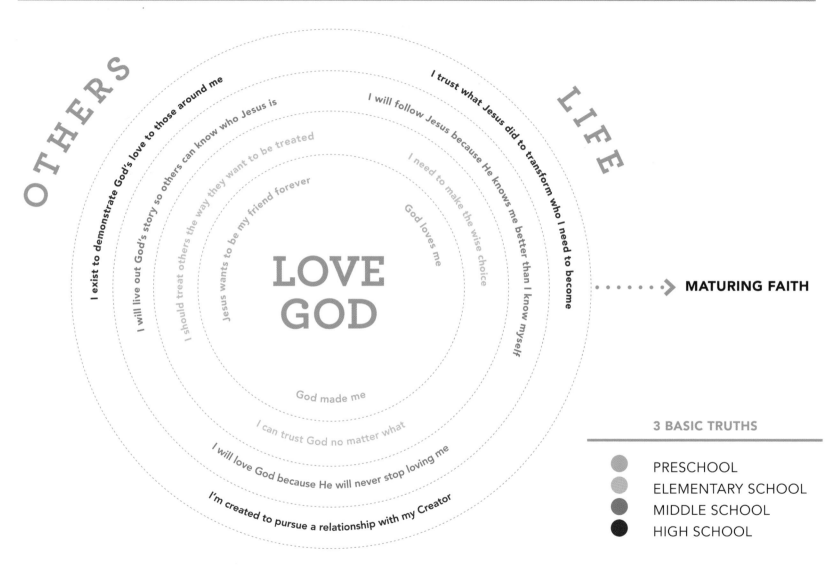

OTHERS

LIFE

I exist to demonstrate God's love to those around me

I will live out God's story so others can know who Jesus is

I should treat others the way they want to be treated

Jesus wants to be my friend forever

I trust what Jesus did to transform who I need to become

I will follow Jesus because He knows me better than I know myself

I need to make the wise choice

God loves me

LOVE GOD

God made me

I can trust God no matter what

I will love God because He will never stop loving me

I'm created to pursue a relationship with my Creator

GOD

······> **MATURING FAITH**

3 BASIC TRUTHS

● PRESCHOOL
● ELEMENTARY SCHOOL
● MIDDLE SCHOOL
● HIGH SCHOOL

When you recycle what is most important, it amplifies your message across other platforms.

It helps you strategically . . .

partner with every parent so core messages are reinforced at family time.

focus every communicator so they stay aligned.

rally every volunteer to reinforce the same weekly big ideas.

You can't make kids show up more consistently.

You can't make more hours in the week.

So you need to make the time you have matter more.

When you recycle what matters most, you add more voices.

An important part of your strategy should be to get everyone saying the same thing at the same time.

When you identify the handful of essential, need-to-know, life-changing core insights that kids need to grow up believing, then it's easier to add more voices. Make sure you are posting, printing, videoing, sending, painting, and singing these messages to create as many platforms as possible to say what you need to say. You reinforce your message to have a more lasting impact when parents, small group leaders, presenters, musicians, pastors, and volunteers all say the same thing at the same time.

When you recycle what matters most, you add more understanding.

Remember the goal of teaching is not to cover a lot of material, it's to cause someone to learn. Don't be confused by the leader who says, "This needs to be deeper." Be sure they define what "deep" means before you change what you are doing. Deeper is not determined by how many passages have been memorized, or how much of the Bible has been taught. That's why we sometimes call this idea "Teaching Less for More." Teaching less for more can actually be the deepest way to teach, especially if you are helping kids master a concept or truly understand something about God that will affect their life. If you have to make a choice between learning the names of the twelve tribes of Israel or what Paul teaches about grace and forgiveness, go with Paul.

When you recycle what matters most, you add more relevance.
Your core message should be repeated in a rhythm and style that connects with every kid at every phase. Relevance is using the culture around us to say what is timeless. Whenever you leverage what is happening in a kid's own world, you automatically increase their potential to learn. If you are going to talk to preschoolers about how God made the world, why not do it in the spring when the school is talking about Earth Day and their parents are taking them to the park? If you are going to talk to teenagers about moral purity, why not do it in February or March before spring break, prom, and swimsuit season?

A FEW THINGS TO ANTICIPATE
There are a few things you should anticipate if you are really focused on teaching kids what matters most at every phase. When you teach less for more, it means you have to decide what you are not going to talk about. You may decide to leave out the story of Solomon threatening to cut the baby in half when you are talking to four-year-olds, or the story of Jesus casting out demons when you're teaching second graders.

Unless you explain your strategy, there may be adults . . .
who wonder why you are leaving something out,
feel like you already covered this topic several months ago,
or want you to teach something more often than you already are.

**Just remember, you shouldn't prioritize your content based on how adults feel.
You need to prioritize based on how kids learn.**

What if a Kindergarten teacher got tired of teaching the alphabet
and was ready for a little Shakespeare?

What if a dad was tired of throwing a plastic baseball to his toddler,
so he got a real one instead?

Sure, it can seem monotonous teaching the same thing year after year,
but it's the way kids learn. They learn through creative repetition.
(Think about how many times a kid will watch the same movie, or replay the same song.)

That's why every leader has to think about more than just a curriculum.
Every leader needs a strategy for their message.

With a strategy, you can say what matters most,
in a way they will hear it and remember it,
and know what to do about it this week.

"SPIRITUALITY IS DETERMINED BY HOW WELL ONE LOVES, NOT HOW MUCH ONE KNOWS."

ANDY STANLEY

....

THE BUILDING BLOCKS FOR A COMPREHENSIVE MESSAGING STRATEGY

....

(WHAT IS THE SAME AT EVERY PHASE)

1. The Organizing Factor

The primary idea that drives content across a comprehensive strategy

It is reflected in every phase. The Great Commandment is an example of how the right organizing factor should be big enough to connect every message to one thing. It links the content that is being taught at every phase with the overarching goal of learning how to love God.

2. The Relational Motives

Key relationships that become the catalyst for what you teach

The Great Commandment clearly defines relational motives. Remember you are turning three dials constantly. Everything you teach should help kids love God, others, and themselves.

3. The Scriptural Insights

Primary insights that will shape a kid's view of God, others, and themselves

These are the most crucial core beliefs based on Scripture, so you define and redefine them in a number of ways throughout the life of a kid. Although they are not described in terms the average kid would repeat, they run in the background to serve as a guide for what you teach.

(WHAT IS UNIQUE AT EVERY PHASE)

4. The Basic Truths

Specific memorable phrases you want kids to know and never forget

These phrases are crafted so every age group can understand or articulate them. They sum up what authentic faith can look like at different phases. Creating a common shared language in a kid's environment makes it easier for leaders and parents to promote and communicate what kids need to remember.

5. The Personal Responses

Practical applications of truth that help kids at every phase win in their everyday lives

Kids need to know how it matters before it will matter. That's why you need to connect insights and principles to a kid's real world. They need to know what it looks like when someone reflects God's image and follows Jesus.

6. Content Calendar

The organization of bottom lines or key truths into an annual schedule

This allows leaders and parents to visualize the big picture of how the content fits together. It helps everyone know where they are—including parents—and prepare for what's coming next. It provides a tool to evaluate if the messages are being effectively recycled and emphasized at every phase.

7. Optimal Environments

Physical spaces and key events that happen for every age group

An effective "scope and cycle" also recycles what matters through the programming elements that are outside the typical weekly routine. For example, camps, retreats, and discipleship weekends can give leaders significant additional influence in the life of a kid.

Oh, one more thing that influences everything:

Guiding Values

The DNA of a comprehensive strategy

These values are the internal operating system that influences how leaders teach and program for all the age groups. Many of these concepts represent the tensions necessary to build a healthy strategy effective for a wide spectrum of kids. They provide consistent standards that affect every phase comprehensively, and a common language keeps everyone aligned. These values drive many of the decisions on how content is packaged, themed, and presented. Some examples of Guiding Values include the following:

All Scripture is equally inspired, but it's not all equally important or applicable.

The Bible is all true, but all truth is not in the Bible.

What you want a kid to know this week should be connected to what you want them to know this year.

What you say doesn't matter because it's true, it matters when it matters.

If you don't allow your kids to process their own doubt, they will never own their own faith.

Fight for the tension between what is true and what is real so kids won't grow up and reject what is true.

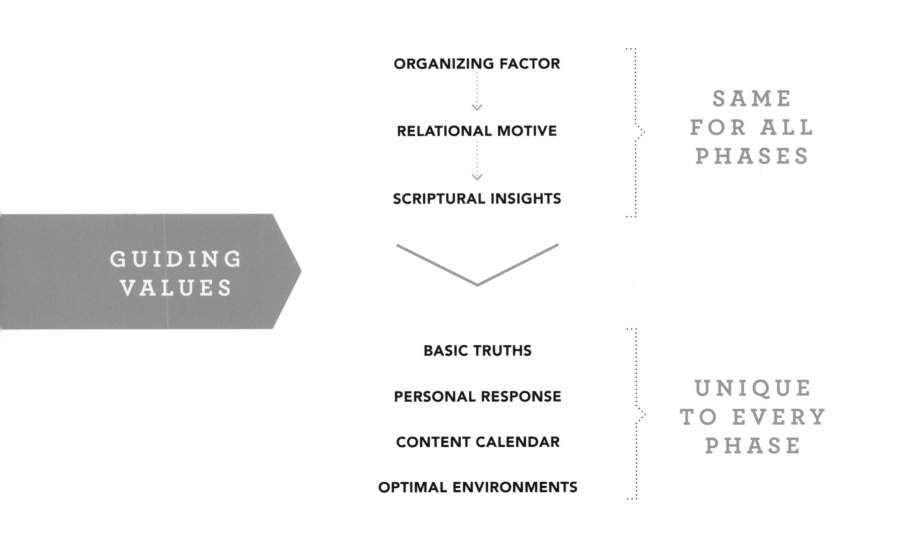

ORGANIZING FACTOR

RELATIONAL MOTIVE

SCRIPTURAL INSIGHTS

SAME FOR ALL PHASES

GUIDING VALUES

BASIC TRUTHS

PERSONAL RESPONSE

CONTENT CALENDAR

OPTIMAL ENVIRONMENTS

UNIQUE TO EVERY PHASE

THE GOAL FOR EVERY PHASE IS THE SAME

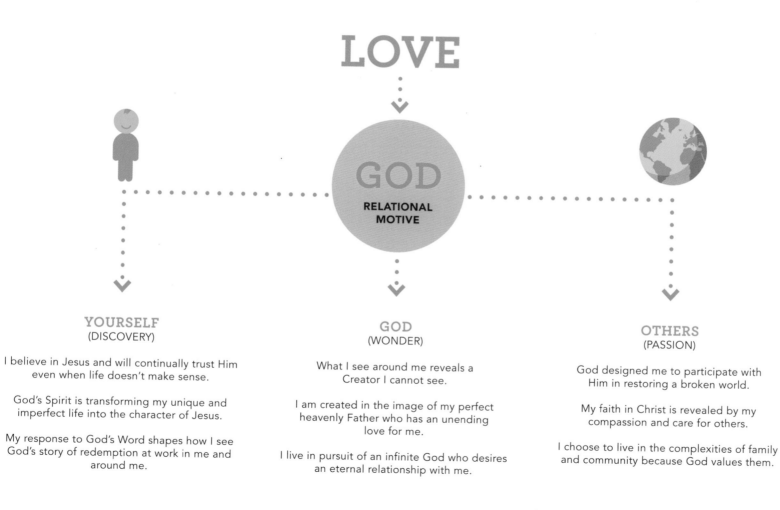

LOVE

GOD

RELATIONAL MOTIVE

YOURSELF
(DISCOVERY)

I believe in Jesus and will continually trust Him even when life doesn't make sense.

God's Spirit is transforming my unique and imperfect life into the character of Jesus.

My response to God's Word shapes how I see God's story of redemption at work in me and around me.

GOD
(WONDER)

What I see around me reveals a Creator I cannot see.

I am created in the image of my perfect heavenly Father who has an unending love for me.

I live in pursuit of an infinite God who desires an eternal relationship with me.

OTHERS
(PASSION)

God designed me to participate with Him in restoring a broken world.

My faith in Christ is revealed by my compassion and care for others.

I choose to live in the complexities of family and community because God values them.

YOUR ROLE IN EACH PHASE CHANGES

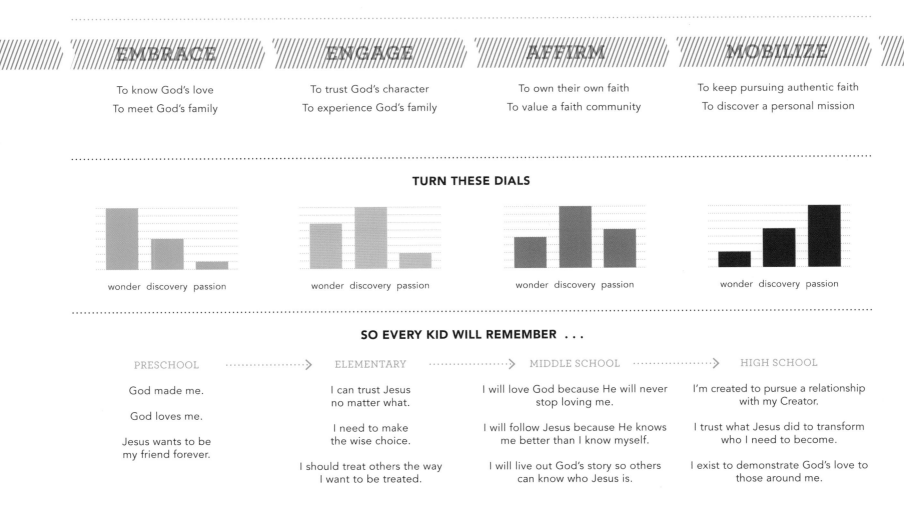

EMBRACE

To know God's love

To meet God's family

ENGAGE

To trust God's character

To experience God's family

AFFIRM

To own their own faith

To value a faith community

MOBILIZE

To keep pursuing authentic faith

To discover a personal mission

TURN THESE DIALS

wonder discovery passion

wonder discovery passion

wonder discovery passion

wonder discovery passion

SO EVERY KID WILL REMEMBER . . .

PRESCHOOL ··········> ELEMENTARY ··········> MIDDLE SCHOOL ··········> HIGH SCHOOL

God made me.

God loves me.

Jesus wants to be my friend forever.

I can trust Jesus no matter what.

I need to make the wise choice.

I should treat others the way I want to be treated.

I will love God because He will never stop loving me.

I will follow Jesus because He knows me better than I know myself.

I will live out God's story so others can know who Jesus is.

I'm created to pursue a relationship with my Creator.

I trust what Jesus did to transform who I need to become.

I exist to demonstrate God's love to those around me.

13

CELEBRATE THE BIG MOMENTS

SO KIDS AT EVERY PHASE WILL PAUSE AND REFLECT ON WHO THEY ARE BECOMING

Every phase has a past, present, and future.
That's what makes the phases *phases.*
They are windows of time that pass by.

Another way to say it is this:
Every phase builds on yesterday's foundation
to maximize the opportunities of today
so we will have a better story tomorrow.

In this way, our life builds like the plot of a story where two things are true at the same time.

What happens consistently over time builds the character of our story.
What happens in a moment can change the direction of our story.

Some of our most lasting memories come from everyday moments. Think about what you remember from your own childhood. Maybe it's a smell from the kitchen, or the feel of the weather in a certain season, or a particular song.

Some of the most impactful moments happen on significant days. If you were to write out the story of your life, these would be the moments that moved your story forward in one direction or another. The day you were born. The day you trusted Jesus. The day you got your first job.

When it comes to the next generation, what if there was a way to celebrate significant days in a way that made them even more significant?

Think about holidays, birthdays, family traditions, and milestones. These big moments have unique potential unlike any other day.

Big moments are an opportunity to . . .
celebrate our history,
clarify our present,
and imagine our future.

Big moments are also an opportunity to . . .
remember God's faithfulness,
celebrate God's presence,
and anticipate the future fulfillment of God's promises.

That's why the Israelites celebrated feast days and why Jesus served the last supper. They knew the potential these moments have to connect us to a bigger story.

It's God's story.   It's my story.   It's our story.

IF EVERYDAY MOMENTS
ARE THE PAGES OF OUR LIVES,

BIG MOMENTS ARE THE
TURNING POINTS IN THE STORY.

One of the easiest ways to *miss* the big moments is to overdo them.

**If you celebrate too soon or too often,
you risk making the big moments smaller.**

Don't celebrate too soon.
There is power in anticipation.

That's part of what this book is about. In an increasingly on-demand, instant culture, it's easy to want to rush into what's next. But childhood can't be rushed. If we forget how significant a phase really is, we may unintentionally rush children into the next phase before they're ready. In doing so, we not only miss the opportunities of the present phase, but we steal from the coming phase as well.

Don't celebrate too often.
Frequency has a diminishing return.

If you ate cake every night after dinner, birthdays wouldn't taste as sweet.
If you kept a decorated tree in your living room all year, Christmas wouldn't feel as warmly lit.

No one understands better than Disney how to keep the magic alive.
That's why they invented "the Disney Vault."

You know, the Disney Vault. It's that impenetrable lockbox that stands between your child and his or her favorite animated movie. As frustrating as it is when the secret agents of Disney Inc. are guarding your favorite classic, it's actually a brilliant concept. It's more than a marketing scheme. The Vault ensures that the classics have life for future generations.

The principle is simple.
Delayed gratification is more gratifying.

So, just remember.
If you make every moment a big moment,
there may not be any moments big enough.

That's the reason some middle schools decide not to have a "graduation ceremony."
It's okay to save some things for later so they can actually matter when they matter.

Another way to miss the big moments is to confuse them.

All big moments aren't equal. If we confuse what is unique about different kinds of celebrations, we may miss the distinctive opportunity for each one.
Think about these three categories.

Grade Level Promotions (happens annually)
Events that celebrate and introduce someone to the start of a new phase

Promotions and parent orientations aren't the only thing your ministry will do for parents, but they're definitely a significant time you should leverage annually to re-engage parents in your strategy. Use this opportunity to train your parents about the present and upcoming phase of their child. Give parents a plan for the year and explain how you hope to support and partner with them over the next twelve months.

Shared Traditions (happens seasonally)
Events that celebrate customs and practices which will be passed from one generation to the next

Birthdays and holidays set a rhythm for the year. Whether they are celebrated in the home or in the church community or both, these moments provide an opportunity to tell our story. They remind us of what matters. As a leader, look for practical and meaningful ways to leverage significant calendar events. Share those with parents and leaders in your ministry. Help them establish or enhance a few traditions.

Life Stage Milestones (happen once in a lifetime)
Events that mark and celebrate a significant moment or change in a person's story

Of all the moments to celebrate, these are the moments that matter most. They are the milestones. They happen only once in a person's life. They happen on a specific day. They are determined by the individual family, not the calendar. The next pages will talk specifically about the potential of six life stage milestones that happen from birth through graduation.

BEGINNING (baby dedication)
WISDOM (first day of Kindergarten)
FAITH (salvation or baptism)
IDENTITY (coming of age)
FREEDOM (driver's license)
GRADUATION (well, you get it)

The number of milestones you celebrate may vary. Maybe you have five. Maybe you have seven. If you start adding to this list, just remember more isn't better. These moments will have greater potential as six milestones than they will if you create eighteen. Every year shouldn't be a life stage milestone any more than every day should be National Doughnut Day.

Every one of the life stage milestones involves family, and at least three of these milestones are traditionally celebrated in the church. Life stage milestones are always celebrated in community. Maybe that's because it's hard to karaoke without an audience, or because most cakes aren't sold by the slice. There are at least two other good reasons to celebrate these moments in the context of relationships.

1. Life Stage Milestones help kids discover their personal identity.
With each life stage milestone, kids have an opportunity to pause and reflect. And in that moment, relationships act like a mirror. The people who know a kid best have the most potential to show a kid who they have been, who they are, and who they are becoming.

Imagine every child has a sign that reads,
"I see me when I see the way you see me."
Or a more complicated version might be this,
"I see me the way God sees me when I see you see me the way God sees me."

When you celebrate a life stage milestone, you invite adults and peers to stop what they are doing not only to celebrate, but also to reflect back to a child or teenager what they see. What the community says in these moments sends a powerful message to reinforce something about that child's personal identity.

2. Life Stage Milestones mark a change in our position.

Whether it's a baby just entering into the community or a kid making a public profession of faith, every milestone marks a change in a kid's role within the community. Just like a change in any relationship, it's helpful when everyone acknowledges it.

Otherwise, it would be like . . .
moving into the corner office when no one discussed your promotion.
telling your deepest secret to someone who didn't know you were friends.
showing up at Thanksgiving with a new wife no one knew about.

When you celebrate a life stage milestone, you invite the entire community to come together and make a public declaration. Something significant has happened, and it's worth noticing. What they celebrate in this moment validates the new role this person has within the community.

Simply put:
A milestone marks a change in my story and our story.
A milestone celebrates a change in who I am and who we are.

The next pages are a synopsis of the distinctive opportunity of each of the Six Life Stage Milestones.

LIFE STAGE MILESTONES

BEGINNING

**CELEBRATING THE FIRST
CHAPTER OF LIFE**

The beginning of a child's life is a time for parents to identify their community, to surround themselves with support, and to imagine the end for their child. A baby dedication is a moment in time when parents publicly commit to parenting with the future faith of their child in mind.

WISDOM

**CELEBRATING THE POTENTIAL
TO DISCOVER AND LEARN**

The beginning of formal education is an opportunity to celebrate the accomplishments of toddlerhood and tell stories that highlight a child's growing character. The first day of school is also a moment in time when parents can communicate their hopes for their child's future choices and discoveries.

LIFE STAGE MILESTONES

FAITH

**CELEBRATING THE DECISION
TO FOLLOW CHRIST**

A baptism is a moment in time when a child or teenager makes a public profession of faith. In that moment, parents, relatives, peers, and the wider church community celebrate their decision to trust Jesus. It is also an opportunity to establish spiritual habits that will support future spiritual growth.

IDENTITY

**CELEBRATING THE JOURNEY
TOWARD ADULTHOOD**

A coming-of-age celebration brings dignity and intentionality to an otherwise awkward life transition. It's an opportunity to identify critical influences in the life of a preteen, to surround them with support, and to imagine the end for their child. A coming-of-age celebration is a moment in time when parents and adult leaders affirm a preteen and share the secrets of living an adult life with faith and character.

LIFE STAGE MILESTONES

FREEDOM

**CELEBRATING A SIGNIFICANT
STEP TOWARD INDEPENDENCE**

The day a teenager gets his or her driver's license marks a significant change in their level of independence. A driver's license is a moment in time when parents can celebrate one specific accomplishment and communicate their hopes for their son or daughter's future choices and continued freedom.

GRADUATION

**CELEBRATING THE TRANSITION
TOWARD VOCATION AND CAREER**

The end of basic education marks the end of a significant era in a person's life. Graduation is a moment in time when parents re-tell the stories of the phases of a teenager's life. It's a moment to identify core relationships that will advance with a teenager as they transition toward a new life with vocation and career.

LIFE STAGE MILESTONES

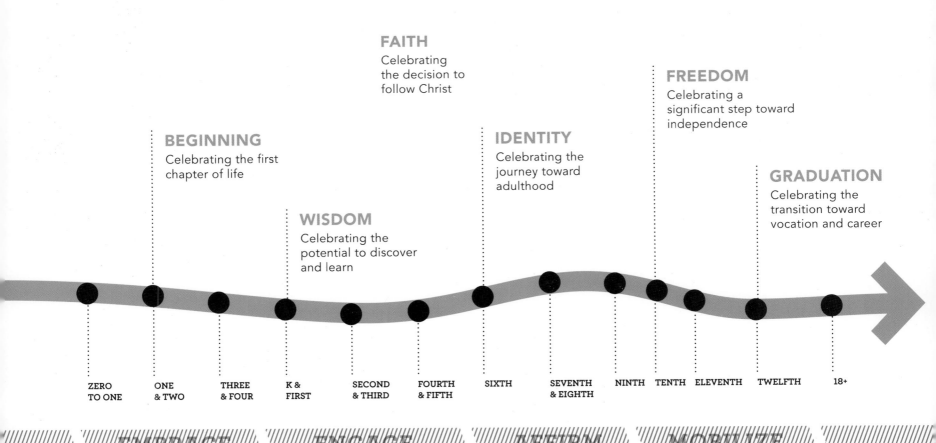

FAITH
Celebrating the decision to follow Christ

FREEDOM
Celebrating a significant step toward independence

BEGINNING
Celebrating the first chapter of life

IDENTITY
Celebrating the journey toward adulthood

GRADUATION
Celebrating the transition toward vocation and career

WISDOM
Celebrating the potential to discover and learn

ZERO TO ONE | ONE & TWO | THREE & FOUR | K & FIRST | SECOND & THIRD | FOURTH & FIFTH | SIXTH | SEVENTH & EIGHTH | NINTH | TENTH | ELEVENTH | TWELFTH | 18+

EMBRACE   ENGAGE   AFFIRM   MOBILIZE

PHASE TIMELINE OVERVIEW

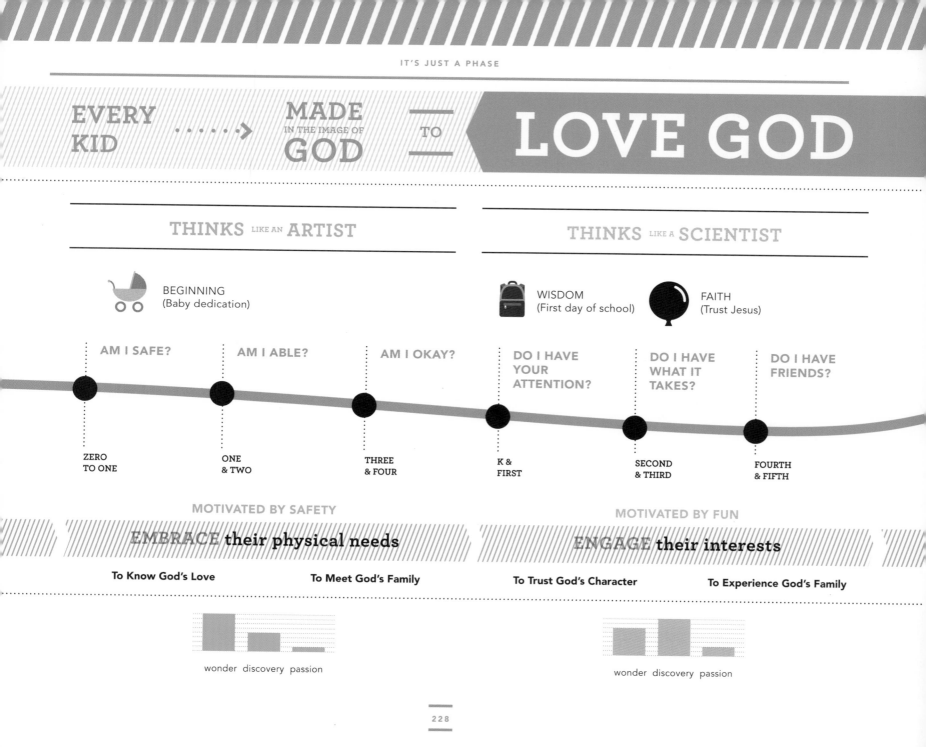

EVERY KID ·····> MADE IN THE IMAGE OF GOD — TO — **LOVE GOD**

THINKS LIKE AN ARTIST

THINKS LIKE A SCIENTIST

BEGINNING
(Baby dedication)

WISDOM
(First day of school)

FAITH
(Trust Jesus)

AM I SAFE?	AM I ABLE?	AM I OKAY?	DO I HAVE YOUR ATTENTION?	DO I HAVE WHAT IT TAKES?	DO I HAVE FRIENDS?
ZERO TO ONE	ONE & TWO	THREE & FOUR	K & FIRST	SECOND & THIRD	FOURTH & FIFTH

MOTIVATED BY SAFETY

MOTIVATED BY FUN

EMBRACE their physical needs

ENGAGE their interests

To Know God's Love   To Meet God's Family

To Trust God's Character   To Experience God's Family

wonder discovery passion

wonder discovery passion

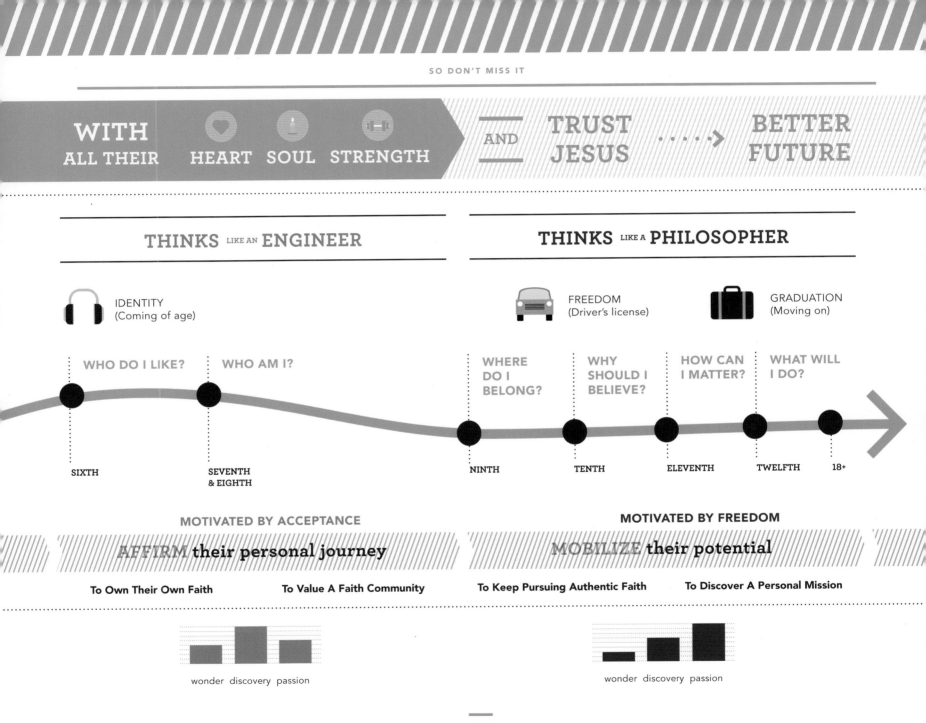

WITH ALL THEIR **HEART SOUL STRENGTH** AND **TRUST JESUS** ····> **BETTER FUTURE**

THINKS LIKE AN **ENGINEER**

THINKS LIKE A **PHILOSOPHER**

IDENTITY
(Coming of age)

FREEDOM
(Driver's license)

GRADUATION
(Moving on)

WHO DO I LIKE?

WHO AM I?

WHERE DO I BELONG?

WHY SHOULD I BELIEVE?

HOW CAN I MATTER?

WHAT WILL I DO?

SIXTH

SEVENTH & EIGHTH

NINTH

TENTH

ELEVENTH

TWELFTH

18+

MOTIVATED BY ACCEPTANCE

MOTIVATED BY FREEDOM

AFFIRM *their personal journey*

MOBILIZE *their potential*

To Own Their Own Faith

To Value A Faith Community

To Keep Pursuing Authentic Faith

To Discover A Personal Mission

wonder discovery passion

wonder discovery passion

EVERY KID
MATTERS

Jesus had a pretty high opinion about kids.
Remember, He actually said, *"Whoever welcomes one such child in my name welcomes me."*

In other words,
"I want you to treat kids like you would treat me.
And by the way, just in case you haven't figured it out by now, I am God.
So just make sure you understand when you welcome kids, it's like you are welcoming God."

Okay. That's a paraphrase, but you have to admit,
Jesus made every kid a pretty big deal.

It was like Jesus was suggesting . . .
no one should feel more welcomed at your church than a screaming baby.
no one should feel more welcomed at your church than a bratty kid.
no one should feel more welcomed at your church than a hormonal middle schooler.
no one should feel more welcomed at your church than a defiant teenager.

So what if they don't . . .
sound like God.
act like God.
smell like God.

You should welcome every kid and every teenager as if you were welcoming God.

Why?

Because . . .
they are made by God.
they reflect the image of God.
they have potential to love God.

And if there's one thing Jesus modeled for us clearly, it was that the people who follow Him should welcome everyone. Jesus positioned Himself as the way to know God, then He threw the door wide open. That's why the Pharisees panicked. They had an identity crisis because there were people walking through the door who didn't look like them.

If everyone in your church is comfortable with who is showing up on Sunday,
you haven't opened the door wide enough.

You can almost hear Jesus saying,
"See those tax collectors, let them in!"
"See those prostitutes, let them in!"
"See that Samaritan woman, let her in!"
"See those Kindergartners, let them come to Me."

The way you welcome
every kid
at every phase
every week
may be the most important thing you do.

There is no other organization, government program, or nonprofit
that can do what the church is positioned to do in the lives of kids and teenagers.

Because we know the Creator,
we can help a kid discover their created potential.

Because we have been welcomed and forgiven,
we can give every kid a place to belong regardless of their failures.

Because we trust in a risen Savior,
we can offer hope for a better future.

When a local church makes the kids and teenagers a weekly priority,
something remarkable happens both in the community and in the church.

That's why . . .

WHAT YOU DO EVERY WEEK MATTERS

If every kid has been made in the image of God,
and every kid matters to God,
then what you do every week in a kid's life matters.

What you do every week in a kid's or student's life
matters more than you think it does.

A preschooler probably won't turn your lesson into a meme on Instagram. Just because there isn't a lot of
immediate gratitude, that doesn't mean the work is less significant.
You may never see the results -------- > those might come in a different phase later on.
You may not know how to measure success ------ > some days the conversation may lack a little depth.

But every week, the way you . . .
embrace a preschooler,
engage an elementary school kid,
affirm a middle schooler,
and mobilize a high schooler
has the potential to radically change their future.

What you do every week in a kid's life now
will matter more than what you do for them as adults.

That may sound like an overstatement, but it's actually true.
What you do for a kid matters more because it's like any other investment—it gains shares.

Simply put,
deposits in the life of a child earn more interest.
When you wait until they are adults, the gains are slower.

What you do every week in a kid's or student's life,
will keep your church from dying.

That may just sound mean, but it's the reality in more ways than one.

Kids and teenagers will keep your message focused.
(You will never realize the importance of prioritizing your message
until you have to communicate it to a room of middle schoolers.)

Kids and teenagers will keep your environments relevant.
(You never have to ask for their opinion.)

Kids and teenagers will keep your doors open.
(There is no way to send a more powerful message to your community,
than to care for the kids they care about.)

What you do every week in kids' lives
will probably change you more than it does them.

Yes, in some ways working with kids will make you feel older,
but when it comes to your . . .
faith,
perspective,
and tech savvy,
spending a few hours every week with kids will help you grow.

What you do every week in a kid's or student's life
will last a lot longer than you do.

You will die one day.
Chances are you won't even have a campus named after you or an article written about you in *Time* Magazine.

But what you do for kids and teenagers now will leave behind a legacy
so that one day they will do for the generation behind them what you did for them.

That's how a spiritual legacy is passed from one generation to the next. That's how the church moves from today into tomorrow with a message of faith and hope and love.

So . . .

WHAT YOU DO AT EVERY PHASE MATTERS

It's just a phase . . .
So don't miss it.

The crawlers in your preschool won't be crawling next year—some might even be potty-trained.
The fourth graders in your community won't be fourth graders next year—well, a few might be.
The seniors who are still coming to your church might not be next year—some might have a job.

These phases pass by more quickly than we realize.
But every phase in a kid's life matters.

And because every phase matters, you have a responsibility to
influence significant relationships in every phase so kids will know they matter.

That means you should . . .

influence every influencer that can potentially impact what's happening at every phase of a kid's life, and give every leader and every parent a simple and clear role so they can embrace, engage, affirm, and mobilize kids toward a better future.

Because every phase matters, you have a responsibility to
understand how kids are changing in every phase
so you can be effective at moving them in a positive direction.

That means you should . . .
never stop learning everything you can learn about how kids are changing mentally, physically, culturally,
relationally, emotionally, and morally, and never stop applying what you know to how you do ministry.

Because every phase matters, you have a responsibility to
leverage the distinctive opportunities of every phase so kids will feel loved
in a way that radically changes the way they love God, themselves, and others.

That means you should prioritize what matters in a way that every kid will hear it and remember so they will walk
away and know who God is, and what it looks like to love and trust Him this week.

The more you show up every week to model love
and become familiar with what is happening in a kid's life at every phase,
the more opportunity you have to nurture a kid's faith.

Every phase gives you a new window of time
to help kids rediscover who God is and relate to Him in a unique way.

Why?

Because every kid is created in the image of God.
Because every kid is designed to mature in how they relate to God.
Because every adult has a unique opportunity to demonstrate how God loves kids.

When you show up in the lives of kids at every phase,
it helps them see what God's love and forgiveness actually looks like.

That's what Jesus did.

Jesus treated everyone like they were made in the image of God.
Jesus redefined for everyone what it means to love God.
Then Jesus showed everyone how to be forgiven.

**That's why Jesus challenges those of us who follow Him
to open the door wide enough so every kid
can know they are invited to follow Him too.**

SO YOU DON'T MISS IT . . .

Okay. That's a lot of information to take in all at once . . . or maybe you already knew it all. Either way, what does any of this *really mean* for your ministry? Practically speaking, how do you influence significant relationships, understand present realities, and leverage distinctive opportunities so you can help kids have a better future?

There are many answers to that question, but here is a checklist of some things that will be true in your ministry if you want to make the most of every phase.

1. Every age group in the church has a specialist who champions them.

2. Age-group specialists meet regularly as a team to discuss comprehensive issues.

3. There is a seat representing next generation ministries at the executive leadership table.

4. Age-group leaders have a simple and realistic annual plan to learn more about their age group (development, culture, pressures, etc.).

The plan may include a mixture of the following: read books, listen to podcasts, subscribe to a leadership site, follow blogs, meet with other specialists in your community (educators, counselors, nonprofits), or attend a conference.

5. Age-group leaders use their understanding of theology and child development to design environments and plan production elements.

6. Your next generation ministry has one clear and comprehensive strategy for helping parents win at every phase.

7. Next generation ministries share the responsibility of recruiting and training weekly small group leaders for every age group.

8. Age-group ministries have an annual parent orientation to tell parents what they need to know about the phase of their child, and about how your church can help them over the next 52 weeks.

9. Age-group ministries have a weekly strategy to communicate with parents and provide simple resources to help them reinforce the message at home.

10. Age-group ministries have an annual orientation for small group leaders to tell them what they need to know about the phase of their group, and how you will help them lead over the next 52 weeks.

11. Age-group ministries have a weekly strategy to communicate with small group leaders and provide resources to help them connect with their group.

12. Age-group curriculum cooperates with a comprehensive strategy to understand what has come before and prepare for what will follow after.

13. Every age group has a scope and cycle that prioritizes content around what is more important for that particular phase.

14. Age-group leaders collectively own a strategy for celebrating critical lifestage milestones, both in the church (Baby Dedication, Salvation/Baptism, Graduation), and in the home (first day of school, coming of age, driver's license).

15. Age-group leaders leverage phase specific lifestage milestones to connect with the family, celebrate each kid's story, and promote future spiritual growth.

One more thing . . .
Every leader in the church values every phase and treats every kid who breathes like they are made in the image of God.

THE PHASE PROJECT IS A COLLABORATIVE EFFORT

We want to say a special thank you to those who have not only done research, given hours of their time, and debated words and phrases, but who have also made a lifetime commitment to helping kids and teenagers grow in faith so they can have a better future. You can also look for new Phase resources coming soon from the authors in bold.

Jon Acuff
Anna Aigner-Muhler
Sarah Anderson
Mawi Asgedom
Frank Bealer
Jessica Bealer
Sharai Bradshaw MA
Sarah Bragg
Jim Burns
Elle Campbell
Abby Carr
Elizabeth Carswell
Crystal Chiang
Mike Clear
Sam Collier
Ben Crawshaw
Holly Crawshaw
Lydia Criss Mays PhD
Jackie Dunagan LMFT
Mallory Even LPMT, MT-BC
Alexa Felice
Amy Fenton

Doug Fields
Brad Griffin
Pam Haight
Stuart Hall
Elizabeth Hansen
Kathy Hill
Mike Jeffries
Donny Joiner
Darren Kizer
Kacey Lanier
Caz McCasslin
Laura Lenz MT-BC
Brooklyn Lindsey
Cara Martens
Nicole Manry PhD
Laura Meyers PhD
Sue Miller
Paul Montaperto
Lindsey Needham
Ben Nunes
Brandon O'Dell
Greg Payne

Kara Powell
Kevin Ragsdale
Hannah Rinehart MA, LPC, NCC
Nina Schmidgall
Dan Scott
Grace Segars
Tom Shefchunas
Angie Smith
Deborah Smith MA, LPC
Deb Springer
Sherry Surratt
Colette Taylor
Lauren Terrell
Melissa Thorson
Autumn Ward
Jim Wideman
Chinwé Williams PhD, LPC, NCC
Jon Williams
Melanie Williams
Jennifer Wilmoth LMFT
Karen Wilson

AUTHOR BIOS

REGGIE JOINER

Reggie Joiner, founder and CEO of the reThink Group, has journeyed through the phases with four kids of his own. He and his wife Debbie raised Reggie Paul (RP), Hannah, Sarah, and Rebekah, and now they're well into the phases not covered in this book.

The reThink Group (also known as Orange) is a non-profit organization whose purpose is to influence those who influence the next generation. Orange provides resources and training for churches and organizations that create environments for parents, kids, and teenagers.

Before founding the reThink group in 2006, Reggie was one of the founders of North Point Community Church. During his 11 years with Andy Stanley at North Point, Reggie was the executive director of family ministry where he developed a new concept for relevant ministry for children, teenagers, and married adults.

Reggie has authored and co-authored ten books including *Think Orange*, *Seven Practices of Effective Ministry*, *Parenting Beyond Your Capacity*, *Lead Small*, *Playing for Keeps*, *Creating a Lead Small Culture*, and *Zombies, Football and the Gospel*.

For more information about Reggie Joiner, visit ReggieJoiner.com or connect with him on Twitter @ReggieJoiner.

KRISTEN IVY

Kristen Ivy, executive director of messaging at Orange, and her husband Matt are currently parenting through the phases. Their Kindergarten son, Sawyer, and preschooler, Hensley, were in the room while most of this book was being written. Their third child, Raleigh, raced this book to the presses and was born just as this book was released.

Before beginning her career at reThink in 2006, Kristen earned her bachelors of education from Baylor University in 2004 and a Master of Divinity from Mercer University in 2009. She worked in the public school system as a high school Biology and English teacher, where she learned firsthand the joy and importance of influencing the next generation.

At Orange, Kristen has played an integral role in the development of the elementary, middle school, and high school curriculums and has shared her experiences at speaking events across the country. Kristen is a co-author of *Playing for Keeps* and *Creating a Lead Small Culture.*

Kristen lives in Cumming, Georgia, with her husband Matt. For more information, visit KristenIvy.com or connect with her on Twitter @Kristen_Ivy.

ENDNOTES

The research data in this volume is collected from individual interviews, academic resources, and group conversations around the "It's Just a Phase" concept. Some of the specific findings are found on the following pages:

[1] Catherine Stonehouse, *Joining Children on the Spiritual Journey: Nurturing a Life of Faith* (Grand Rapids: Baker Academic, 1998), 70

[2] Francis E. Jensen with Amy Ellis Nutt, *The Teenage Brain: A Neuroscientist's Survival Guide to Raising Adolescents and Young Adults* (New York: HarperCollins, 2015), 48, 51

[3] Leslie Haley Wasserman and Debby Zambo, *Early Childhood and Neuroscience: Links to Development and Learning* (Dordrecht, the Netherlands: Springer), 62

[4] Clea McNeely and Jayne Blanchard, *The Teen Years Explained: A Guide to Healthy Adolescent Development* (Baltimore: Johns Hopkins, 2009), accessed 21 March 2015 at http://www.jhsph.edu/research/centers-and-institutes/center-for-adolescent-health/_includes/interactive%20guide.pdf

[5] Shapiro, Lawrence E. *How to Raise a Child with a High EQ: A Parent's Guide to Emotional Intelligence* (New York: Harper Perennial, 1998), 54